Fire and Ice

Human-centered and Mechanistic Paradigms in Software Design

Fire and Ice

Human-centered and Mechanistic Paradigms in Software Design

Derek Kelly

Writers Club Press
San Jose New York Lincoln Shanghai

Fire and Ice
Human-centered and Mechanistic Paradigms in Software Design

Writers Club Press
an imprint of iUniverse, Inc.

For information address:
iUniverse, Inc.
5220 S. 16th St., Suite 200
Lincoln, NE 68512
www.iuniverse.com

ISBN: 0-595-20548-8

Printed in the United States of America

To Tony Stuart, guru,
and to
Joe Frick and Bert Prospero who went with the flow

Contents

Preface ix

Acknowledgements xvii

Introduction xix

Chapter 1 Requirements for a POD System 1

Chapter 2 POD System Design using the Ice Paradigm 12

Chapter 3 POD System Design using the Fire Paradigm ..51

Chapter 4 Explanation of the Fire and Ice Paradigms 94

About the Author 115

Index 117

Preface

Human-centered software design is one of the major topics of conversation and discussion in academic computer departments as well as in software development enterprises. Everyone is talking about it. Yet, there is rampant confusion in these circles over just what human-centered design is. Some people seem to think that human-centered software systems are those at which human factors experts are thrown, or those where task analyses are performed and are used to inform the development process.

My sense is that fundamental to the design and development of human-centered software is a particular **mode of thought**, a specific way of thinking about and doing software design. I wish to provide evidence in support of this thesis in this book.

The book describes two types of software design philosophies that produce or result in two different types of software systems. One design philosophy, designated as the ice paradigm in this book, dominates the current software development industry. The other design philosophy, which I think is much more suitable for human-centered computing systems and that I call the fire paradigm, **should**, I believe, come to dominate the industry.

This book is the result of reflections on my experiences in computer software development. It is not an academic treatise on software design. Nor does it describe any software development process or methodology. You will hear nothing about methods, or classes or b-tree searches or focus items here. I have nothing to say about Windows or Unix or Mac, or any other operating system competing for a niche in the marketplace.

What you will find here is a **story** with fairly detailed descriptions of two fundamentally different types of software design philosophies that I have encountered in the software industry, one that I call the fire model and the other the ice model. These models or paradigms are described in more detail in the Introduction. Briefly, the ice paradigm is mechanistic and emphasizes structure over function, while the fire paradigm is more human-centered and puts the primacy on function rather than structure.

Author's Background

In my first career, I spent a dozen years teaching logic and philosophy to university students. Bitten by the personal computing bug in 1976, I then spent the remaining twenty-five years of my working life working on various and sundry software development teams for a dozen different companies mainly as a technical writer, though I had started out in the industry as a programmer and systems analyst.

My initial foray into technical writing for the software industry was for an oil and gas system whose users pelted the staff with a daily barrage of help calls because they did not have any documentation. Once we had some documentation, those calls were reduced almost 1000 percent. That was what convinced me to continue working to produce documents that explained and illustrated, in clear and simple terms, complex operations for ordinary, non-technical users.

I have worked on around a dozen software development teams developing documentation in oil and gas systems, financials, marketing, human resources, production control and other systems using both personal computing as well as mainframe platforms on Unix, Windows, and others. I have thus been exposed to a wide variety of software development methodologies and approaches.

In the course of my work on software teams, I have had the privilege of working with at least two geniuses in the field. My first major project in the early 1980's was documentation for the Comprehensive Manufacturing Control System (CMCS), supported by STSC, Inc. of Rockville, Maryland. Robert Goodell Brown, at one time a member of the IBM Board and the inventor of statistical techniques like exponential smoothing that is used in production and inventory control environments, developed this system in APL. My final project, in 2000, was working with a workflow group led by Tony Stuart, one of the people to whom this book is dedicated, who developed systems for IBM that instantiate the fire model of software design that I describe here.[1]

Aim of the Book

One of the crying needs in the software development industry is for interfaces between users and computing machines that are user-centered or human-centered. This means in part that computer application systems should assist users in doing their work instead of forcing users to conform to a machine and its requirements.

My principal aim in the book is to provide somewhat detailed descriptions of what I believe are the two main paradigms or models of software design. I want to describe the kinds of systems or applications that their design strategy results in creating. I believe that one is better than the other when trying to create human-centered systems, and I shall show why I think this to be the case.

I think that what I call the ice model of design has to this point dominated the software industry, to its detriment. If the industry is to really develop and produce human-centered computing systems, it is going to have to adopt a fire model of design. I therefore hope to produce a document

1.   This is my interpretation only. Mr. Stuart may or may not agree with anything I say in this book.

that ordinary people can use to petition the leaders of the software industry to develop their software using a model different from the one they ordinarily use.

Who this book is Written for

The book should be of interest to anyone who has ever used a computer, particularly a personal computer to perform some work task, be it writing a memo or controlling a production system. In other words, this book is primarily for **users** of computer application systems. Such users may then be able to point to this book to explicitly require of their developers and software vendors the type of software design they prefer and need.

The book should also be of interest to software developers, from project leaders to programmers, as well as to software gurus and managers, for it shows the consequences and benefits of using one or another of the two types of software design methodologies. Though they will learn nothing about programming techniques or algorithms here, they may be interested in seeing the differences between a human-centered design method and a machine-centered design method.

Organization of the Book

The book is organized into four chapters. Chapter 1 sets the stage by describing a set of requirements for a software application for an imaginary company. These requirements are then given to two different sets of developers to design a system that implements the requirements. The idea is that the customer will select one of the two systems to use in their business.

One team, described in Chapter 2, develops a system using the ice paradigm; the other team, described in Chapter 3, develops a system using the fire paradigm. In both of these chapters, I describe the systems analysis and design of the systems. I also describe the type of documentation associated with each type of system and how they are used. Chapter 4 then provides a theoretical explanation of the differences between the two types of software design and wraps up the book by considering the role and place of each of the two types of design in human-centered systems.

Conventions

This being the Internet age, I have provided URLs (links) to sources of information rather than printed materials. I have left out the http prefix because most, if not all, browsers automatically add that prefix to any address the user enters. All such references are used for illustrative or informational purposes only and do not imply my endorsement or recommendation of the services offered by any of these links.

Terms separated by a | indicate a path or sequence of selections from a menu, for example File|Open means open the File menu and select the Open command.

Except for the three fictional companies mentioned in this book, all other company names or products mentioned in this book may be trademarks, registered trademarks or service marks of their respective owners.

Acknowledgements

I would like to thank the following individuals, many but not all of them from IBM who reviewed some of the material contained in this book or provided invaluable feedback and knowledge about some of the topics discussed here: Brian Doyle, designer extraordinaire, Joe Frick, Ray Knudson, Scott Mastie, and Bob Niemitalo who provided a key insight into finite state machines.

I am also indebted to Elsbeth Sweeney and Doug Ward, great managers and wonderful people who put up with ye old curmudgeon. I'd also like to thank Wesley Isenhart and Eric Rice for their collegiality. I owe Amber Grimes thanks for a great place to work, and Brian Lee for providing a source for a writing necessity.

Introduction

In this introduction, I want to explain what the title of the book means by describing the meaning of the words in the title.

Paradigms

A paradigm is an exemplary instance of something. So, an exemplary soldier, for example, would be someone who exhibits and has exhibited all or most of the virtues of soldiering in their lives and work. Being a paradigm implies that the person or thing so indicated can serve as an example of how to be like the paradigm—be and do as he or she or it does.

The word "paradigm" was popularized many years ago by Thomas S. Kuhn in his book, *The Structure of Scientific Revolutions*,[2] where he argued that certain programs of scientific research have tended to dominate now one and now another era of science. As he used the term, a paradigm of

---

2. Published by the university of Chicago Press in 1962

science was an entire program of research including practitioners, methods of analysis, the design of experiments, and the principal discoveries and hypotheses of the sciences.

In this book, I am using the word paradigm to denote a mode of thought or a way of thinking that underlies activities and guides intellectual tasks. I have found in my twenty plus years of experience in software development that the teams I have been associated with tend to fall into two kinds of groups, each one of which seems to be dominated by a peculiar way of doing software design work. The fire and ice metaphors are thus used to point to a sort of world-view that function as underlying assumptions of software design. These ways I am calling paradigms.

Fire and ice are two real-world metaphors that I use throughout this book to characterize what I think are the two principal forms of design in the software industry, two paradigms of software design. The fire and ice paradigms appear to be pervasive in the industry and to compete with each other for the "soul" of software developers.

The two paradigms of fire and ice result in different ways of responding to software system requirements, different ways of doing system analysis and design, and correspondingly different ways of documenting and using the systems that result from their work.

These paradigms of software design have nothing to do with the size of software development teams as I have found the paradigms at work in both large and small teams. Similarly, they have nothing to do with the process that is used as I have found both paradigms at work in teams that follow a strict process as well as in those that follow a haphazard methodology.

Metaphors tend to be bendable only so far and then they break, that is they cannot support the weight of concepts placed upon them. Nevertheless, I want to try to explain what the metaphors mean to me in this book and thus hopefully make them meaningful to you, the reader.

The Ice Paradigm of Software Design

We all know that cold and heat are two of the dominant features of the universe. Cold tends to inhibit or restrict life and action, while heat is needed for life. Scientists have identified a condition, called absolute zero, where all motion ceases—where it's so cold that nothing happens, where there is no change, development, or motion of any kind. Hence, not even a photon can escape since bodies emit photons only when they are hotter than their surroundings.

In the history of thought, I find that there is one individual who has portrayed the universe as a cold one in the sense in which I am using it here. Parmenides was a Greek thinker born in 651 BME who wrote a poem called *On Nature*[3],

---

3. See home.ican.net/~arandall/Parmenides for a translation of this poem.

where he described all that exists (the universe) as something in which there is no development, for the universe is immutable and unbounded. The final sentence in the poem, for example, states that "One and unchanging is that for which as a whole the name is: 'to be.'"

In his poem, he enunciates a principle, which is that anything rationally conceivable must exist. This means that there is nothing more to an entity or an existent than its structure. Development, or change or flow or movement of any kind is a derivative feature of existents. The universe is thus a static entity, a body at rest and in complete equilibrium.

Whether or not Parmenides would have used the metaphor of ice to characterize his view of things is not my concern here.[4] What is of interest here is that I am using the ice metaphor to characterize a paradigm of software design where structure is paramount over function and where, in effect, function is a derivative of structure.

This is a paradigm of software design where the structure of the software is primary over the function, where the static elements (the structure) dominate the function (the movement) of the application. Thus, when I speak henceforth of the ice paradigm, I mean one where structure is paramount and function is derivative. Of course, if a software application

---

4.   See pages.prodigy.net/jmsn/cosmology.htm where the author argues for a cosmology based on the idea of a big freeze rather than a big bang. I have no idea about the validity of this cosmology.

were designed with the conditions of absolute zero in mind, there would be no function or dynamism at all.

The Fire Paradigm of Software Design

In a condition of absolute zero, there is only one thing that can get anything moving—the application of heat. The structure formed by water in crystalline form can be broken by heat, and fire (or sunlight) is our most immediate and natural experience of heat. Unlike the static phenomenon of ice, heat is a dynamic phenomenon—one that consumes fuel and produces heat, light, and other effects.

Heraclitus, who preceded Parmenides, was another Greek thinker who wrote a treatise on the universe, where he characterized the cosmos as being fire eternal. "This cosmos," he said, "always was and is and ever shall be ever-living fire." In the history of thought, Heraclitus is the fire thinker whose universe is one where one can never "step twice into the same river" for all things are in constant flux and change.

Though the sun may be our most immediate and pervasive experience of heat, fire is our proximate experience of the phenomenon. Fire consumes energy while also producing effects (like heat and light). Fire (or heat) generates movement and activity. Unlike ice, fire is a dynamic phenomenon.

In light of these views, I am using the word fire to characterize a paradigm of software design where the emphasis is on function rather than structure, on the flow of work rather than the structure of tasks. When I speak of the fire paradigm henceforth, I shall thus mean a way of doing software design where the principal design elements are workflows or processes rather than structures, and thus where the dynamic elements are primary to the static elements.

The Use of Paradigms in Software Development

I certainly would not want to suggest that software developers and designers consciously choose one or another of these two paradigms whereby to govern their work. On the contrary, I rather think that the paradigm selected for use in a development project is more likely selected tacitly or unconsciously by the designer as a function of his background, environment, and cognitive predilections.

Nevertheless, some cognitive framework guides software design. The result of the design is the application being developed. That cognitive framework determines how the application works and how it is understood and operated by users and even its very appearance.

In this book I want to exhibit what I think are the two dominant cognitive frameworks or paradigms of software design. I want to describe the different designs that result from these frameworks.

The description of these paradigms uses the following approach. All writing involves three elements provided in some order or another is the course of the work. The letters

DEI denotes the three elements of Define, Explain, and Illustrate. My approach in this book is to provide a definition of the two paradigms, fire and ice, as I have done in this introduction, to provide a detailed example of each of the two paradigms (in Chapters 2 and 3 respectively) and then to provide the explanations in Chapter 4.

Chapter 1 Requirements for a Print-on-Demand (POD) System

This chapter describes a project undertaken by a fictional company, the Rothschild Publishing Company (RPC), to develop a print-on-demand (POD) software application system for their business.

The chapter introduces RPC to the reader and describes the system and project requirements. Chapter 2 describes how a software development company analyses, designs, and documents a system that uses the ice paradigm of software design. Chapter 3 describes a system that uses the fire paradigm of software design.

The Rothschild Publishing Company

RPC is an old-line publishing house that is situated in a major US city. For many years, RPC has performed the standard functions of most other publishing houses. It has requested the submission of books for consideration, and accepted some for publication. Those accepted for publication have been placed into a production process, where they have been printed, distributed, and sold to the public.

RPC has editorial and submission offices throughout the world. Like most everyone else, RPC has added computing technology to its offices, and connected everyone to an internal LAN or via the Internet.

Writers submit their manuscripts either in printed format or via the Internet. Communication between writers and RPC is carried out either by e-mail, if that is available, or by ordinary mail.

One of the major decisions that RPC has to make for each book that they publish is the number of copies to print for the initial and subsequent editions. Given the vagaries of the market and the marketability of different types of books, the initial run may vary from 500 to 10,000 copies or more. Since there is no way of determining how many copies of a book will actually be sold, RPC is constantly having to invest capital in risky publications that do not return their investment.

Another of the company's major costs is distributing copies to different distributors, like bookstores, and then receiving payment only for copies sold with the rest returned to the company. Another cost is warehouse space to store copies of printed books and inventory control to keep track of them.

Questions like the following have been constantly on the minds of management personnel:

- How to **reduce** the capital invested in printing books before knowing the demand?
- How to **reduce** the costs of distributing, warehousing, and returns?
- How to **increase** the return on these capital-intensive investments?

Print on Demand (POD)

Over the last few years, RPC has been investigating the possibilities of POD, print on demand, technology. The POD technology consists of a combination of high-speed printing capabilities together with control software. The basic idea is that by using a high-speed, high-volume print-er any single book can be printed and bound, packaged and shipped in a matter of seconds or at most a few minutes. Everything from order entry to fulfillment thus may be done on an "immediate" basis. This eliminates the need to print multiple copies of a book and to store them before getting customer requests. Books may be printed only when requested by customers.

RPC see this technology as holding great promise for reducing the costs of publishing a book by making it possi-ble to print copies only if and when requested by customers. This feature alone would mean that no inventory of books would need to be printed and distributed—and disposed of when returned unsold. The POD technology also holds promise of changing the printing process and thus further reducing the costs of publishing books. Using computerized publishing systems for example would eliminate typesetting.

With the use of associated control software, customer orders can be accumulated and scheduled for printing and fulfillment on any basis required—by the hour, day, or week, and so on. In addition, the management of publishing houses can obtain real-time information about customer orders, the capacity and demand placed upon the printing systems, and the revenue stream.

The Development Project

After considerable internal study and investigation of the POD technology, RPC has decided to change its publishing process from an old-line to a POD system. Along with this change, they wish to make other corollary changes in their business practices.

As a first step to making this change, they have developed a set of requirements for a POD system. These requirements are described in the next section. RPC intends to request bids for developing a system based on the requirements, select two different vendors to develop two different systems, install both at the company site and use them both for a period of one year before deciding on which one to implement on a permanent basis.

System Requirements

RPC envisages a system with a client-server configuration, where clients are scattered throughout the world at various locations, and a system server is located at company headquarters. Depending on the volume and performance requirements, the server should, preferably be a Windows "professional" level machine, though this is not a strict requirement. We could, for example, use a server running Unix.

What we specifically need in the server is performance and reliability. Since business will be conducted on a 24X7 basis, the server must be up and accessible at all times with a minimum amount of off-line or down time. Perhaps a dual server system with disaster specifications on the database (a redundant disk array?) is required.

Client Side Requirements

Because of the extensive investment that RPC has in existing computer technology, RPC requires that the POD system be implemented so that this technology, consisting primarily of Microsoft Windows running on IBM-type PCs, can continue to be used. Since all company personnel are already familiar with the functions of Windows, training costs for the new POD system would be minimized if this existing hardware were to be used. And while RPC is willing to consider the use of software other than Microsoft Windows, our preference is to continue using this technology.

RPC also realizes that a POD system may require that additional terminals be purchased and would prefer that PC-type machines be used since we have an existing long-term purchasing agreement with a hardware vendor.

Users (defined as both external writers and other vendors, as well as internal company personnel) should be able to access the system from anywhere in the world and from any terminal. For security, RPC requests that a userid or logonid and password system be used as well as system controls on what parts of the system any specific user may access and use.

There should be a common user interface for the system. Users should be able to understand how to use all parts of the system if they have been trained to or have experience in using any part of the system. The user interface should be as natural or intuitive as possible—and internationalized so that people in all parts of the world may feel comfortable with the system.

Global and Local View Requirements

Because of the extensive amount of data that will be collected and stored on the system, a critically important requirement is that not only may specific users of the system be restricted from viewing parts of the system (handled by the userid and password requirement), but that the management level users must be provided with global views of the data.

The global data must be accessible only to management level personnel and the data must be presented in a global or aggregate form. Management must be able to access the system through the same interface as other users, but they must be shown aggregate or summary data primarily. Management should, of course, also have access to any of the detail data that they want to see, but global data views are their principal views.

Operating Requirements

This section describes the operating requirements of the POD system. The requirements are presented roughly in the order in which they are used.

There will be a centralized server, with LAN-attached workstations through the company system. On the periphery will be LAN or WAN or Internet connected workstations as well as access through the Internet for writer submissions, queries, and reports.

Writer Submissions, Queries and Reports

Beginning on the outer circumference, RPC wants to be able to accept writer submission of documents from anyone, anywhere in the world on a 24X7 basis via the Internet. Documents can be in any acceptable format using any standard word processing system that produces output that can be sent over the Internet (e-mail attachment or FTP).

Writers should also be able to submit queries about their submissions on the same basis, and receive reports or responses on the same 24X7 basis. These reports should encompass their submissions, the current position of their submissions in the production process, customer orders for the resulting books, and related royalty and other statements.

Upon submission of new documents, a whole range of associated data (such as the writer's name and address as well as information about the submitted document) needs to be collected and stored on the server. This data needs to be available for changing and updating by the writer and also available to production and management personnel.

Validation Checking

Upon submission, all documents are to be processed for validation, including a check on the number of words, machine readability, and text language. In most cases, manuscripts (documents) will be submitted as a single document in standard "letter" or A4 size, though we want to be able to accept text that is laid out on any-sized sheet, using any font and formatting style.

Validation testing will consist of a number of yes or no switches, where a no would result in having the document returned to the writer or sending a request for additional information, or a yes would initiate another check.

If a document passes validation processing, it passes to the production-processing phase; otherwise the writer is sent an e-mail or standard letter and the document virtually returned (rejected but not physically returned).

As in all previous and subsequent steps, data need to be collected and made available in the form of reports and updateable forms to writers as well as RPC personnel.

Production Processing

Upon submission to production processing, documents are massaged by in-house software systems that will format the submission into the size book and styles suggested by the writer, assign an ISBN number, determine a price, and develop a time-phased schedule for the production process.

The schedule must be able to be amended throughout the production process so that critical path items can be accounted for (by lengthening or shortening the schedule).

There are a number of steps in the production process, and at each step writers and production personnel need to be able to access data about the document, writer, and the production process itself. These sub-steps are:

- Scheduling
- Formatting
- Cover creation
- Proofing
- Library
- Copies
- Order Ready

Order Processing

Once a book has been through the production process, it is ready for order processing. Orders from customers as well as in-house personnel should be able to be placed from anywhere on the system, including, of course, the Internet.

Upon entry of an order, there needs to be validation checking, then submission of the order to the printing process, including a determination of the schedule (usually the same day) and expected shipping date.

A number of sub-steps are also involved in this phase, including:

- Print Run
- Packaging
- Mailing/Shipping
- Tracking
- Returning

Management Reports

In addition to all the separate functions required, summary or aggregate information needs to be provided in the form of reports that only management personnel may access. Among these should be reports on the number of manuscripts received and processed (including error documents that are returned to writers) on a real-time basis; the number of orders received and in process, again on a real time basis; and related documents summarizing detailed data.

RPC POD Project Decision

Upon completion of the RPC POD Requirements as outlined in the previous section, RPC invited a number of different software vendors to consider the requirements and to come up with a design proposal for implementing the RPC POD system.

RPC explained to all vendors who submitted a proposal that RPC would select two vendors to develop a system according to their own design and development methodologies and that RPC would then implement both systems at RPC and subject them to extensive use for a period of one year. After a year of parallel use of the two systems, RPC would then make a determination of which one of the two, if any, to implement on a permanent basis. The basis of the final selection would be the usability of the system developed. RPC users and customers would make the final determination about what "usability" means.

Two companies were eventually selected to develop test systems, NanoSoft Corporation (NSC) and International Development Media (IDM).[5] Chapter 2 describes the system developed by NSC and Chapter 3 describes the IDM system.

---

5.   Please note that both NSC and IDM are fictional companies and any resemblance to any actual company or software product is purely coincidental.

Chapter 2 POD System Design using the Ice Paradigm

This chapter describes a fictional computer application system for a Print-on-Demand (POD) system developed by a fictional vendor, Nanosoft Corporation (NSC), for a fictional company, Rothschild Publishing Company (RPC). The resulting application system is intended to represent a system developed using what I call the ice paradigm of software design.

The description includes the following aspects:

- System Analysis
- System Design
- Documentation and System Use

Note to the Reader: Any software development project will, at a minimum, involve system analysis and design as well as functional specification documents that may be hundreds of pages long. Add to this the user documents (that are not always included!) and the system documentation may well be several hundreds of pages in total. In this chapter, I will be describing an abbreviated form of these documents. In addition, I will have nothing to say about actual routines that are to be coded. My attention will be focused almost entirely on the user-visible features of the system.

System Analysis

This system analysis for the RPC POD is based upon the requirements described in the previous chapter. The principal aim of this analysis is to develop a list of the system parts or components.

User Analysis

The first step in the analysis is to determine who will be using the system. An understanding of users is necessary for user management, to determine usability criteria, and to manage security and user authentication issues. Configuring who can use the system and what they can use it for is also one of the keys to security of system data.

The RPC POD requirements list the following kinds of users:

- General public
- Managerial
- Order processors

- Production
- Staff (general)
- Writers

General Public

The publisher's Web site will be open to all Internet users. These users can do one of two things on the site. One is to browse books for sale and purchase books. Another is to review the book submission processes and requirements; if a general user decides to submit a book for publication, then they would become a writer and should follow the procedures required of writers.

Managerial

Managerial users will generally be located at the RPC site, though they may be located anywhere and need access to global and detail information from anywhere in the world. Such users will need to be able to access the system both through the Internet as well as from local client machines.

Order Processors

All book orders can be placed via the Internet (by the general public) and so require no RPC intervention. However, orders may also be taken over the phone or by letter or by walk-ins, so the system needs to provide a manual as well as an automated (via the Internet) method of order entry, though the same screens could be used for both purposes.

Production

Production-related staff may be situated either on or off site, as may production facilities. There are a number of different roles performed by production personnel, including:

- Manual or automatic release of daily or weekly queues of manuscripts
- Manual or automatic processing of released manuscripts through the transformation, cover design, proofing and printing phases
- Print scheduling and printer monitoring
- Coordination with the order processing and fulfillment personnel

General Staff

RPC staff members include general administrative, accounting, and support staff some or all of which will be using the system in some role or another.

Writers

Writers will access the system via the Internet or by mail or by walk-in to make document submissions, pay the required fees, track the progress of their submissions through the publishing process, place orders for their books, and track revenues.

Function Analysis

The second step in the analysis is to determine what general functions the users of the system need to perform. The RPC POD requirements supply us with a list of the functions that the system needs to enable users to perform.

- Create and proof covers
- Create and proof documents
- Logon
- Marketing data collection
- Order fulfillment
- Order placement
- Production processing
- Publication
- Query documents
- Query processes
- Reporting
- Sales Tracking and Royalties
- Scheduling
- Submit documents
- Validate submissions

Task Analysis

A task is a series or set of activities that are undertaken to perform some function. For example, the function of creating book covers involves a sequence of actions that are done by at least two different types of users, writers and cover designers.

The purpose of a task analysis is primarily to verify the system requirements by including users in the analysis and design process. Observing and analyzing how users currently perform their jobs, for example, how documents are proofed or how data is collected from writers accomplish this. By taking account of the way users perform their jobs, what the jobs are meant to do, and the cognitive skills involved in doing these jobs, we are able to decompose overall functions into their constituent parts or steps.

Create and Proof Covers

- Writer submits a document for publication, along with cover suggestions, including colors and cover art within the boundaries set forth by the publisher.
- Submitted document must pass validation testing and be accepted by the publisher.
- Upon validation and acceptance, the document enters the production phase. Body text and art goes into the transformation subsystem to format and perform other proof-ready actions. Cover art and suggestions go to the graphics department for cover creation.
- Proofs for both cover and text are sent back to the writer for proof review. Proofed covers and text are then returned to the publisher for final production processing.

Create and Proof Documents

- Writer submits a document for publication, along with cover suggestions, including colors and cover art within the boundaries set forth by the publisher.
- Submitted document and graphics, if any, must pass validation testing and be accepted by the publisher.
- Upon acceptance, the document enters the production phase. Body text and art goes into the transformation subsystem to format and perform other proof-ready actions.
- Proofs for both cover and text are sent back to the writer for proof review. Proofed covers and text are then returned to the publisher for final production processing.

Logon

There are two types of logon procedures, one for writers and one for RPC personnel. Both types involve the assignment of userid and password to each user. Writers login to the system via XHTML forms from the Internet. Internal users login to the system itself. While every user on the publisher's side is allowed access to the system, only management users are allowed access to certain reports.

Marketing Data

When a document is submitted for publication, data about the document, including author's name, publication categories, suitable reader ages, and marketing type blurbs are collected and stored in the database. This marketing data is subsequently used on the RPC Web site to publicize the book.

Order Fulfillment

- Orders enter the system from a variety of places, including book distributors, book sales sites (like Amazon.com), and individual requests submitted through the publisher's Web site. Company personnel may also enter orders manually.
- Upon entry, an order is validated and a ship date assigned.
- The order is then placed into the open item-printing queue.
- When the printing queued is released, manually for expedited items or automatically, the number of copies of the book that were ordered are printed and bound, and enters the outbound queue.
- Books are selected from the outbound queue, automatically or manually, and are wrapped, stamped, and placed into USPS containers, which are picked up on a regular basis.

- Once shipped, the order requesters are billed (e.g., credit cards are invoiced) and the revenue distributed to various places (publisher, writer, distributor, bookseller, and so on).

Order Items

- Orders enter the system from a variety of places, including book distributors, book sales sites (like Amazon.com), and individual requests submitted through the publisher's Web site. Company personnel may also enter orders manually.
- If ordered directly from the publisher, orders immediately enter the order fulfillment phase. If ordered from elsewhere, orders must be sent to the RPC for processing and order fulfillment.

Publication

When a document has completed the production process, it must be published before it can be available for ordering.

Publishing a document involves registering it with Books in Print, registering it with a distributor, and publicizing its availability to selected booksellers. At the same time, the file(s) associated with the document (that has now become a book) must be loaded into the order-processing directory from where it can be retrieved for printing on demand.

Production Processing

Once submitted documents have been validated, they go into the production-processing queue, which has two streams.

One stream has the submitted document as its input and the document formatted for publication as the output. Submission to this process may be automatically or manually initiated. Upon completion, the item goes into its individual directory on the server from where it can be uploaded to the writer's computer for viewing, viewed online directly or viewed by company personnel.

The other production-processing queue stream goes to the graphics department where the cover is created using the writer's direction and the graphic designer's ideas. At the time, the size of the printed book is determined and the exact measurements for the cover and the completed book are determined. Upon completion, the cover is deposited into a document-specific directory (identified by the ISBN number) from where it can be uploaded for viewing on the writer's computer, or printed and mailed to the writer.

Once documents have been formatted and proofed, their two files (one for text and one for the cover) are moved from their proofing queue to the printing queue from where they can be retrieved and printed on demand.

Query Documents

Queries about documents may be made by external agents (such as writers and the general public, for example reporters) as well as by company personnel. Information from the database needs to be made available in the form of packaged reports for this type of user.

Internal company personnel may make queries about documents at any time. Some queries may be packaged as reports, while others may be ad hoc.

Query Processes

Company personnel may make queries about processes at any time in the form of reports or ad hoc queries. Queries about processes are generally available only to writers and others who have an account with the publisher, and to RPC personnel.

Reporting

A set of reports is to be made available on the system. These include reports for various personnel in charge of a specific phase in the production process as well as management summary reports. Most of these reports will be based on data drawn from single tables in the database. Management reports may involve reports based on data from two or more tables, thus requiring SQL joins.

Sales Tracking and Royalties

Once documents have been published, they are available to the sales module. Each sale is tagged as a sale of a particular kind, such as full retail price or discounted by a specified amount for sales to book clubs, booksellers that sell at a discount, and sales to the author.

Except for sales to the author, all sales involve revenue generated for the publisher and a contractual percentage paid on a regular basis to the author. Thus, each sale and each sale price must be tabulated and marked so that royalty payments may be calculated. In addition, any payments must also be registered.

Scheduling

Whenever a document is submitted for publication, an initial schedule is attached automatically to it. This schedule must take account of the different production phases. The schedule must also be capable of being changed as deadlines are met or not.

Submit Documents

The document submission process includes a number of steps, each with a set of data that must be collected and stored (and which can be queried and changed):

- Writer name, address and associated information required for registration and opening of an account with RPC

- Document title, subject matter, number of words, number of illustrations, and cover requirements
- Marketing information including writer bio and book information
- Payment data
- In addition to the above data collection items, the document and all associated data, such as graphics, must be uploaded by e-mail, regular mail or FTP to the publisher's site.

Validate Submissions

Documents submitted for publication must be validated before entering the production process. This is an automatic process that can also be initiated manually. The validation process checks to see that the submitted materials conform to the publisher's guidelines, including the required minimum number of words in the document, content readability, and so on.

Other Analyses

Depending upon time and budget constraints, other forms of analysis may be carried out at a later time. If it is determined that a prototype of the systems needs to be developed and customer tested, motor analysis and link analysis could be performed to help determine the design of individual component functions and tasks.

Similarly, a cognitive analysis could be done after the system has been designed and implemented to help the trainers determine the level of skills and the worker types required to perform the different tasks.

System Design

This design document describes the following items:

- User-interface
- User Management
- Menus
- Data Element Requirements
- Standard Reports

User-interface

As specified by RPC in the requirements document, the client interface of preference is Microsoft Windows with its graphical user-interface (GUI). In keeping with this requirement, the RPC POD system will use the standard Windows interface, whose primary GUI elements are the WIMP factors (windows, icons, menus, and the point-and-click).

Application Window

In keeping with the requirement to maintain continuity with the interface that all current users are familiar with, a standard Windows application window will be used. The application window will have the standard application window structure and appearance.

RPC-POD (in the title area)
Menu bar
Tool bar

(Active Area)

Status bar

The name of the application system, RPC POD, will appear in the normal fashion at the top of the screen. The menu bar will appear in its normal place, followed by a tool bar, then the active area. As usual, the status bar will appear at the bottom of the screen.

Icons

The system will be installed on the RPC server. Client machines will have the RPC POD system icon installed on their desktops.

NSC will retain some of the standard icons on the standard menus on the menu bar (see the following section), and will design icons for RPC-specific functions, where possible. These icons will be associated with the menu items (commands) they are intended to represent.

Menus

The default menus on the menu bar, which are the File, Edit, Windows, and Help menus, will be retained. RPC-specific menus, as detailed below, will be added to the system. These menus will be either single node or multiple node menus. Where multiple nodes are required, a menu command, in standard hierarchical menu fashion, will display a sub-menu.

Some menus like the management reports menu will require userid and password control for access.

Point-and-Click

In standard Windows fashion, the normal point-and-click device, the mouse, will be retained and used. Where necessary, that device can be supplemented by other devices in the same mode, specifically barcode readers for fulfillment verification.

User Management

The front-end of the system manages the different types of users who may access the RPC POD system.

With the exceptions noted in the sections below, the standard user authentication will require that when a user selects the RPC POD icon on the desktop, a login dialog will display requesting a userid and password. Both items will be sent to the server, which will verify them. If either the userid or the password is invalid, the login will be denied. All users will be required to have a userid and password associated with the system.

General Public

The general public will have access to the RPC Web site and no login or password will be required unless a user has an account with RPC for the purchase of books.

Management

Management users, like all users, will be required to have a valid userid and password for general access to the system. In addition, all management users will have a secondary userid and password that allows access to the management-level reports.

Order Processors

Since ordering of books may take place from the Web site or from a system console, there will need to be two order entry screens, one on the Web and one on the system. The one on the system will require a userid and password for access, but the Web-based ordering screen will not have a userid and password.

Production

Production staff will require userid and password for access to the system.

Staff

Members of the staff will require userid and password for access to the system.

Writers

Writers will not have access to the system, but will access their accounts via the Web. Each Internet account will require a userid and a password for access. A writer without Web access may request hardcopy account reports (that will be provided by RPC personnel).

Menus

As is the case in Windows, menus (in hierarchical format) will be used to provide users with the commands they can use to perform system functions.

All the menus will be placed on the standard Windows menu bar. The RPC POD system will retain the four standard application window menus (File, Exit, Window, and Help), but will modify some of the standard functions on these menus, and will add or subtract commands. In addition, we will add four application-specific top-level menus

(Book, View, Order, and Reports) to the menu bar. The following sections describe the top-level menus and the commands they will provide. All associated data items are defined in the next main section below.

File

The standard Windows File menu will be used by the RPC POD system. Some of the standard menu items of that menu will however be modified to fit the application. Since the RPC POD system is a **book** processing system, the commands will be modified to fit this environment. Following are descriptions of the items on this menu.

New Account

Since this is a book processing system, this command will be used to open a new account for a new book for a writer. When accessed from this selection, the system will display XHTML entry forms that collect data about the writer, the book, the audience, payment for the service, and uploading of the book file(s) to the RPC POD servers.

Open Account

This command will prompt the user to enter a writer or author name, a book name or an ISBN number and will display the associated information. This command is used by RPC personnel to browse writer or author accounts. This command may also be used from the Internet and will display the same forms as used in "New Account" but will allow changes to be made.

Close Account

This command is a redundant command, which will also be available on the "Open Account" window.

Save and Save As

The Save and Save As commands will be made available to save any information changed in any function that allows changes to be made. The Save As command will include the Standard options, as well as the option to save the active document as a Web page.

Print Commands

The standard print commands, Page Setup, Print Review, and Print will be included without any modifications.

Send To

Since documents of various sorts need to be sent back and forth among RPC staff, this command will allow the active window to be sent to various destinations.

Edit

The Edit menu will be used and all the standard document-editing commands will be retained and function as they normally do, namely Undo, Cut, Paste, Select All, Find, and Replace.

Windows

The standard Window menu will be retained. It will provide the following standard-function commands: New

Window, Arrange All, Hide Menu, Hide Tools, Close, Close All.

Help

The standard Windows Help menu will be used. It will include access to the standard Windows Help for the RPC POD system, a context-specific help function, access to numbers for the NSC technical support Web pages and numbers, and the About (RPC POD) command.

Book

The majority of commands associated directly with the RPC POD system will be included on this menu. Most of the commands will be used to perform various actions on documents that been received for processing into books. Once a document has been published, its files will reside in the Published directory and will be unavailable for modification. Following is a description of the commands on this menu.

Validate

When a new book document has been loaded into the Pending directory, it remains there until it has been validated positively. If the document fails validation, a bit is set and an e-mail (or a snail mail, if that option was selected by the writer) is sent to the writer with the validation report. If the validation is successful, the file(s) are automatically loaded into the Production directory. Validation may be performed automatically on all new documents, or manually on a case-by-case basis.

Load

Upon receipt from the writer, a document and its associated files are uploaded into the Pending directory. Once through the production process, a book is published into the Published directory. Everything between these two points will be stored in the Production directory. Once a document (and its associated files) has been loaded into the pending directory, the files must be validated (using the Validate command). Once validated, the files need to be loaded into the Production directory using this Load command.

Similarly, when documents have been formatted into publishable books and the proofs are ready to be reviewed, the proofs have to be loaded into the Proof subdirectory of the Production directory from where the writer may download the files for review.

Graphics

For those books that contain graphics, this command will make whatever transformations are needed so the graphics can be merged into the formatted text.

Format Text

When a document or book file has been loaded into the Production directory, the first step is to format the book into publishable form. The cover is created at a separate step. Since a book may be published in several different sizes and formats for printed books, this command will provide a dialog that displays the format the writer requested (and allowing changes, if needed, by RPC staff) then launches the appropriate formatting routines.

Format Cover

This command is used to format the cover for a book. It displays a dialog displaying the writer's suggestions (such as colors, graphics, etc.) and allows changes and additions by the cover designer before launching the cover routines.

Transform Book

Once formatted, a book may be transformed in a number of ways. One way is to transform the publishable proofs into a PDF and to load that into the Proof directory for download and review by the writer. If a book is to be made into an e-book, another transformation needs to be done. If the book is to be viewed via the Web, yet another transform needs to be made. Similarly, there may be a need to send the book out in RTF, PostScript or some other format.

Publish Book

Once a book has been proofed, it can be published. This command will perform a set of functions associated with the publication, including registering it with booksellers and distributors, placing it into the RPC database and Web page, loading the files into the Published directory, and others.

Query

This command will display a dialog requesting the writer or author name, book title or ISBN and will display information about its current status.

View

The View menu will provide different ways of viewing the currently active document or book. It will be available only when a manuscript or book is being worked on; otherwise, it will be blanked out. (This is subject to review, as we may want to let the menu remain active but blank out some of the subcommands. A decision will be made on the basis of a human factors task analysis.)

The commands to be included here are:

- Full Screen
- Zoom
- Toolbar
- Print Layout
- PDF Layout
- Text Layout
- Web Layout

Order

Orders for books may be placed from several sources including direct orders placed over the Web, orders from booksellers, which may also come in over the Web as batched orders, and internally placed orders. While it is expected that most order-placement will be performed automatically, this menu will provide manual equivalents for the automatic processes. Following is a description of the commands on this menu.

Place Order

This command will display standard book order entry forms for the input of data and the placing of the order into the shopping cart for subsequent payment processing. Included here is an option to place a hold on an order until the hold is released (by a date, a time, or a user action).

Check Orders

This command will display a dialog box requesting entry of the query criteria (for example, orders for all books for today, orders for a specific book, and so on), then will launch the appropriate routines.

Check Schedule

Like the previous command, this command displays a dialog requesting the criteria (book, printer, and so on) then launches the appropriate routines.

Reports

This menu will provide access to a list of reports for the system. Many reports will be available to any RPC staff member. Some management-level reports, however, will be password protected so that only those with the appropriate password will be able to view them. These reports are described in detail in the section following next below.

Data Element Requirements

This section describes the database tables that will be used by the RPC POD system. Other than system tables, six database tables will be required for the system: writer, book, royalty, order, production, and publish. This section describes the layout of these tables.

The next main section describes the standard reports that will be derived from these tables. These tables will be defined as tables for a relational database such as Oracle or DB2. The examples shown in what follows are based on Oracle SQL.

Note to the Reader: For obvious reasons, the following tables are only partially defined and characterized. In addition, instead of using side tables to represent various status values, the status values are shown in the main table.

Book

Assuming that the Book table has already been defined in the database and that SQL is running, the command

SQL> desc book

returns:

Name	Null?	Type
ID	Not null	Number(5)
Author	Not null	Varchar(30)
Title	Not null	Varchar(50)

ISBN	Not null	Char(10)
Pubdate		Date
Listprice		Number(6)

Order

The order table holds information about customer orders for a book.

SQL> desc order

returns:

Name	Null?	Type
ID	Not null	Number(5)
Author		Varchar(30)
Title		Varchar(50)
ISBN		Char(10)
Listprice		Number(6)
Copies		Number(5)
Custlname		Varchar(30)
Custfname		Varchar(30)
CustAddr		Varchar(50)
Custpayform		Char(2)
Custpayno		Char(12)
Custbtotal		Number(8)
Custship		Number(8)
Custgrandtot		Number(10)
Custshipto		Varchar(50)

Shipscheddate	Date
Shipactdate	Date

Production

The production table holds information about a book only so long as it is in the production process. The information is used mainly for production process control.

SQL> desc production

returns:

Name	Null?	Type
ID	Not null	Number(5)
Author	Not null	Varchar(30)
Title	Not null	Varchar(50)
ISBN	Not null	Char(10)
Servicename		Varchar(20)
Submitdate		Date
Validationdate		Date
TextFormatdate		Date
Covformatdate		Date
Proofsent		Date
Proofreturn		Date
Proofcorrect		Date
Finalprod		Date
Publication		Date

Publish

The publish table contains information about a published book, including information about whether or not various organizations, like booksellers, have been informed about the book.

SQL> desc publish

returns:

Name	Null?	Type
ID	Not null	Number(5)
Author	Not null	Varchar(30)
Title	Not null	Varchar(50)
ISBN	Not null	Char(10)
Pubdate		Date
Listprice		Number(6)
Contractexpiry		Date
Royaltypct		Number(2)
Booksinprint		Date
Booksellers		Date
Availforsale		Date

Royalty

The royalty table holds information about royalties paid and owed the author. Since this is mainly an accounting table, the table is not further defined and no related reports are provided here.

Writer

The writer table holds information about the writer of a book. Since a book may have more than one author and one person may author more than one book, this table has a many-to-many relationship to the book table. Thus, one record is stored for each book and author.

SQL> desc writer

returns:

Name	Null?	Type
ID	Not null	Number(5)
Lname		Varchar(30)
Fname		Varchar(30)
Address		Varchar(50)
SSN		Char(12)
Title		Varchar(50)
ISBN		Char(10)
Cowriter		Varchar(30)
Editor		Varchar(30)
Imprint		Varchar(20)
Pubdate		Date
Listprice		Number(6)
Royaltypct		Number(2)
Numfree		Number(2)
Numsold		Number(8)
Agreement		Date

Agreeexpiry	Date
Multbookseqno	Number(2)
Notes	Varchar(4096)

Standard Reports

This section describes the reports that will be included on the Reports menu. Most of these reports get their data from one of the tables defined in the previous section. Those management reports that will use password protection will also be noted.

Note to the reader. The SQL in some of the following examples are not necessarily valid as executable SQL for in some case only the intent (pseudo-code) is provided in the example.

Book

The book report displays items that are in the book table. It answers the question, what books do we have in our inventory? When this report is selected, a dialog will request the criteria, which will be a date or date range or year (default to the current month), author name or all (default), ISBN or all (default), and price (default is blank).

The following SQL selects all records by default.

SQL> select distinct * from books;

ID	Author	Title	ISBN	Pub	Price
1	Albright	US Foreign Pol	0111222220	1/1/02	60.00
2	Clinton	Life with Perks	0222333330	2/1/02	75.00
3	Doe	Poor in the US	0333444440	3/1/02	15.00

This report selects all attributes from the books table and lists them in alphabetical order, showing the author, book title, ISBN, publication date and retail price.

Orders

The orders report displays the contents of the orders table. It reports on the number of orders by day, week, month or year for a selected book or for all books.

The following SQL selects the listed attributes.

SQL> select distinct id,author,title,count copies, copiesxprice from orders;

ID	Author	Title	Copies	Total$
1	Albright	US For	1	50.00
2	Clinton	Life	1	60.00
3	Doe	Poor	3	45.00

This report retrieves selected attributes from the orders table, including one aggregate attribute (the count of the number of copies sold) and one calculated attribute (copies x price to arrive at the total attribute).

Production

The production report displays all items currently in production process, by default. A dialog allows the user to specify criteria for selecting records.

SQL> select id, author,title,isbn,submitdte,pubdte from production;

ID	Author	Title	ISBN	Submit	Pub
1	Albright	US Foreign Pol	0111222220	6/1/01	1/1/02
2	Clinton	Life with Perks	0222333330	6/2/01	2/1/02
3	Doe	Poor in the US	0333444440	8/3/01	6/1/02
4	Franklin	Famous Recipes	0444555550	11/1/01	
5	Kohak	Phenomenology	0555666660	12/1/01	

This report displays a selected number of attributes from the production table. This report shows the time lag between the submission date and the publication date.

Publish

The publish report displays data from the publish table showing various dates related to each published book.

SQL> select id, author,title,isbn,pubdte,availsale from publish;

ID	Author	Title	ISBN	Pub	Availsale
1	Albright	US Foreign Pol	0111222220	1/1/02	1/20/02
2	Clinton	Life with Perks	0222333330	2/1/02	2/15/02
3	Doe	Poor in the US	0333444440	6/1/02	7/05/02

This report displays selected attributes from the publish table. It shows the difference between the publication date and the date when the book is available for sale. Like the previous report, this report could be used for analytical purposes.

Royalty

This report is not described in this document.

Writer

The writer report reports on data from the writer table.

SQL> select id,lname,fname,isbn,pubdte,listprice,numsold from writer;

ID	Last	First	ISBN	Pub	Listpr	Numsold
1	Albright	Madeline	0111222220	1/1/02	60.00	300
2	Clinton	Bill	0222333330	2/1/02	75.00	500
3	Doe	John	0333444440	3/1/02	15.00	100

This report displays selected attributes from the writer table. It could also have contained a calculated attribute for the total revenues by book (list price x num sold).

Summary

The summary report aggregates data from the previously described tables. This report is for management and is password protected. Additional reports similar to this one may also be provided.

ID	No Writers	No Books	Copies Sold	Gross Revenue
1	3	3	800	57,000

This summary report is derived by aggregate SQL functions from previous tables. It's the type of report that a CFO would love to see on a regular basis, perhaps broken down by day, week, month and year.

Development

The preceding system analysis and system design sections (including a great deal more detail) would then be turned over to the programmers so they could code and implement the system. Also included here would be testers and human factors and human-centered interface (HCI) experts who would assist in the development of specific routines and functions.

User Documentation

Now that the RPC POD system using an ice paradigm has been developed, documentation for the system is finalized.

This section describes the procedures used to process documents into books.

Writer Data

A writer will submit a document for processing by accessing the RPC POD Web site. Five sets of entries are required:
- Writer information
- Document information
- Audience information
- Payment information
- Uploading of the document and associated materials (e.g., graphics)

When the writer loads all of the above material, the system (1) deposits the document and associated files into the Pending directory, and (2) writes an e-mail to RPC informing them of the upload.

RPC Validation

Each day, an RPC representative will examine the received documents.
- Access **File|Open Account** and entering the name of a writer. The representative needs to check this material to make sure that it is readable and complete. If it is, the document files are sent to the Validate directory automatically when the option is checked.

- Once all pending documents have been checked, access the **Book** menu and select the **Validate** command. A list of documents in the Validate directory will be displayed. Select one or all documents to launch the Validation routine. Those documents that pass validation are sent to the Format directory; otherwise, they are returned to the Validation Failed directory along with a listing of the reasons for failure. You will need to examine the failures and send a letter or e-mail to the writer on what has to be done to correct the problem(s).

- When the problems have been corrected, access the Book menu and run the Validate command. After that, access the **Book** menu and select the **Load** command. A list of all documents in the Re-Validate directory will be shown. Select one or all items and upload them to the Format directory.

Production

At this point, production personnel would take over.
- A production staff member needs to access the **Book** menu, and select the Graphics, Format Text, and Format Cover commands for each set of documents in the Format directory and perform the respective processing.

- Once a document and all associated materials have been processed, the material is loaded into the Proof directory. An e-mail is automatically sent to RPC and to the writer informing them that the proofs are ready for review.

- When the review is completed, a member of the production staff needs to access the **Book** menu and select the appropriate graphics, text or cover commands to make corrections. Once the corrections have been made, the writer and RPC are again informed.

- Once the proofs are satisfactory, access the **Book|Load** command and load the material into the Production directory.

- Periodically, a member of the production staff needs to access the **Book|Publish** command and select one or all items in the Production directory to process documents into books.

Examples and References

Limiting ourselves only to the world of personal computers running Windows, just about any application that is available on the market illustrates this approach to system design. Any application from Microsoft, including Windows, was developed using an ice paradigm. The same can be said for Corel and many other vendors. However, since the ice paradigm is endemic in the software industry, one is likely to find ice systems just about anywhere—I've

seen several under Unix, for example. Chapter 4 delineates
the characteristics of ice systems and these can serve as criteria for identifying them.

Chapter 3 POD System Design using the Fire Paradigm

This chapter describes a fictional computer application system for Print-on-Demand (POD) developed by a fictional vendor, International Development Media (IDM), for a fictional company, Rothschild Publishing Company (RPC). The resulting application system is intended to represent a system developed using what I called in the Introduction the fire paradigm of software design.

The description includes the following aspects:

- System Analysis
- System Design
- Documentation and System Use

Note to the Reader: Any software development project will, at a minimum, involve system analysis and design as well as functional specification documents that may be hundreds of pages long. Add to this the user documents (that are not always included!) and the system documentation may well be several hundreds of pages in total. In this chapter, I will be describing an abbreviated form of these documents. In addition, I will have nothing to say about actual routines that are to be coded. My attention will be focused almost entirely on the user-visible features of the system.

System Analysis

The following system analysis for the RPC POD is based in part upon the requirements described in Chapter 1.

Introduction

The IDM software development team has examined the RPC requirements (described in Chapter 1) and has determined that further clarification of these requirements needed to be done before undertaking a system design for the RPC POD system. The following sections describe the result of these clarifications.

The first item of note in the requirements is the RPC requirement for 24X7 service. Increasingly, all businesses are moving to a 24X7 model. Essentially, this means that revenues and profitability for these businesses depends on pass-through or on the volume and efficiency of their product processing.

RPC's business is processing documents (from writers) into books that are available for sale to the public. While it is obvious that the RPC book-production process is not a **hard** real-time one like air or ground traffic control systems, the process can be classified as a **soft** real-time one very much like a manufacturing process or a banking system.

RPC's business depends on getting documents (from writers) and processing them into books as quickly and efficiently as possible. Time is money. The more efficiently that RPC processes documents into saleable books, the better their business. It is, therefore, IDM's intention in this software development process to focus on the RPC process and on how best to provide automated tools to support and improve that RPC process. To implement this focus, IDM intends to perform an analysis of the current RPC process, then analyze how that process can be re-engineered into a new and improved process.

Workflow Analysis

To assist IDM in determining where automation may be used to support and improve the RPC process, an analysis of the dynamics of their work needs to be undertaken. While IDM has made use of the requirements that RPC has provided, IDM has supplemented these requirements with other documents from RPC (such as organization charts, strategic plans, and business objectives) as well as interviews with and observations of the performers in the RPC process.

Since it is apparent that the RPC POD system can be cast as a time-phased soft real-time system, our first task is to analyze the workflow of RPC to establish the flow of work and the sequence of tasks.

Vocabulary

To understand the following workflow analysis a few concepts need to be defined and understood. Work can be described by the use of three basic concepts—event, actor, and object. An actor is either a user or a software utility that performs work. An object is the item upon which an actor exerts some effort. An event is a specific result that occurs from an action on an object.

An activity is a **set** of events that derive from the work of one actor. A process is a set of activities with a common purpose. A trigger is something that causes some activity to be performed. A workflow, then, is a set of activities (a process) that are related to each other by a trigger event. Each workflow has an initial condition that has no prior event that is relevant to the system, and a terminal condition. Each activity is conceived as a transaction wherein a set of operations is performed on data in a relational database that treats the actions involved in the activity as a single event. The result of a transaction is a trigger event for a subsequent activity.

The RPC Process

The RPC process is a set of activities that are performed on documents received from writers to process them into books that can be sold. The RPC process is thus one with the purpose of generating revenues both from writers, who sub-mit books for publication, as well as from the general pub-lic, that purchases books. The overall goal of the process is to maximize the revenue generated in these two ways and to minimize the costs of generating that revenue.

RPC Activities

The RPC process is composed of or analyzable into a set of activities. This section describes these activities.

- The **initial situation** in the RPC process is a writer who decides to submit a document (and its associated files) to RPC for publication.
- The initial **activity** in the RPC process is the submis-sion by the writer of a document and all associated information (such as writer name and address, docu-ment title and objective, audience, number of words, format, cover design, and graphics) together with a validated payment to RPC.
- Upon successful submission of the above data and document files (generally done via XHTML forms on a Web site and FTP for the files), an event is triggered at RPC to **validate** and evaluate the submission. If the validation fails, the submitted material is returned (virtually) to the writer either as a terminal event (submission is rejected) or a pending event (where the writer must make some changes to the submission and re-submit). If the validation passes, the writer is

informed and the submission passes into the format activity.

- The **format** activity is triggered by the successful validation of a submission. At this point, one or more actors perform the format function to design a cover and format the text (and graphics, if applicable) for a book.

- Completion of the format activity triggers a message (generally via e-mail) to the writer accompanied by instructions on obtaining the proof material and performing a **proof** review.

- Upon completion of the proof review, the writer returns the proof form to RPC (generally via e-mail or snail mail). This event triggers the **correction** activity. If there are no corrections to be made, the book is passed to production. If there are corrections to be made, the correction activity is performed and the proofs returned to the writer for another review.

- The completion of the correction activity triggers the **production** activity. At this point, the book is processed into a POD book.

- Completion of the production phase triggers a number of events. The writer is informed that the book is available for sales. RPC is informed that revenues from the sales of books may be expected and the writer's royalty accumulation activity is initialized. Booksellers are informed of the availability of the book for sale.

Order processing is informed that orders for books may be undertaken.

- The sale of a book triggers the update of the writer's and RPC's accounts.
- The terminal date for the writer's agreement with RPC for a specific book or any other reason for terminating an agreement triggers the end of the writer's account for a specified book at RPC.

Activity Analysis

The previously described workflow analysis provides us with a set of triggers and events that characterize the activities in the RPC process.

1. Submission triggers validation
2. Validation triggers formatting
3. Formatting triggers proofing
4. Proofing triggers correction
5. Correction triggers production
6. Production triggers availability
7. Availability triggers accounting and booksellers
8. Sales trigger accounting and revenues for writers and RPC

Termination triggers cancellation of account

User Analysis

The previous activity analysis provides us with a list of the users for the RPC process, which are:

- Writers
- Validators
- Formatters
- Proofers
- Correctors
- Producers
- Accounting
- Booksellers
- RPC management

These users are really roles that users may play. A role should not be associated with any specific user since the role a user plays at any one time may vary.

System Design

The following design of the RPC POD system is based upon and derived from the preceding analysis of the RPC workflow, activity analysis, and user analysis.

Finite State Machines

The previous analyses indicate that the RPC workflow resolves into a series of very simple deterministic finite state machines. A finite state machine is characterized by a finite set of states consisting of a start state, a small set of transition states and a terminal state all of which have transition conditions and a related transition function.

That the RPC POD system can be characterized as an FSM or a series of FSMs is obvious from the fact that there is a finite set of states through which the RPC process traverses. There is also a finite set of event categories and triggers, and a finite set of actions associated with the transition between states.

In diagram form, we have a process that looks like this.

- (Submission)—>
- —>(Validation)—>
- —>(Format)—>(Proof)——>(Correction)
  —>(Production)—>
- —>(Availability)—>(Sales)—>
- —>(Termination)

Each of the words in brackets can be considered a state; submission is the initial state and termination is the final state. In between, we have three sets of states. One set of states is involved in the initial submission and validation of the submission. Another set of states is involved in the process of getting a document published. The third set of states are involved in the process of selling the finished product.

The initial state, submission, has no prior state (as far as the RPC POD is concerned). The terminal state, termination, has no subsequent state. Each of the other states can be characterized as a simple FSM with an in-basket and a set of activities followed by a transaction that terminates the state. In diagram format, this would appear thusly.

Input (from previous state)—>(State)—>Output (to next state)

The RPC Process

A more detailed description of the RPC process, with the states indicates in brackets, is thus as follows.

- (Submission) triggers the (Validation) state that is ended by a positive validation and a database transaction that records that success and changes the state of the FSM to (Format).

- Successful (Validation) triggers the (Format) state that is ended by a successful format and a database transaction that records that success and changes the state of the FSM to (Proof).

- A successful (Proof) triggers the (Correction) state that is ended by a successful correction and a database transaction that records that success and changes the state of the FSM to (Production).

- A successful (Production) triggers the (Availability) state that is ended by a successful (Sale) and a database transaction that records that success and leaves the state of the FSM at (Sales) until a (Terminal) state is indicated and all sales or other transactions concerning a book cease.

From the previous analysis, we can envision the RPC POD system as a set of interoperating state machines. As designed by IDM, the RPC POD system thus consists of a small set of FSMs that interoperate to provide automation to key parts of the RPC process.

Data Elements

Since each state, except the first, will be triggered by a database transaction that transitions the state into the next (or another) state, the design of the database and data elements will be tied to the states of the RPC process. This section describes the states, their data elements, and the transactions that cause a transition from one to another state.

Two types of database tables will be described. One type is a table that collects data and provides a view of the overall status of the activities in the RPC process. Each state in the process will also have at least one distinct table that is used to collect, store, and report on the steps of the processing in a specific state.

States in the Process

The distinct states that are represented in the RPC POD system are the following.

- Submission

- Validation
- Format
- Proof
- Correction
- Production
- Availability
- Sales
- Termination

Global Process Elements

When a document is submitted to RPC, three actions occur as a single transaction (that is, the database is written to as a single event)—an order number is assigned, an ISBN number is assigned, and the totality of the data submitted by the writer is written to the database.

The order number is unique and can never be changed once assigned. The ISBN number is unique but can be re-assigned to another writer and book if the submission is rejected. The data submitted (including the document and its accompanying elements like graphics) remains in the database unless the document is rejected.

As we have indicated in the previous analysis phase of the project, there are a number of distinct states involved in the RPC process. We can further characterize each state as having certain steps. Each state will be assigned the same set of steps, which are ready, end, in process, and suspended. Whenever an activity is concluded, the database is updated to reflect that fact by setting the end step of the current state and setting the ready step in the next state.

The transition of a book from one state to the next will be accomplished by event listeners (probably written in Java) that will periodically poll to see if any items are in the end step for a state and if so move them to the ready step in the next state. For this reason, there may be a short time gap between the times an item is marked as in the end step of one state and when it enters the ready step for the next state.

A global state and step table will be used to chart the progress of a document or book as it proceeds through the RPC process.

State and Step Table

Name	Null?	Type
ID	Not null	Number(10)
OrderNo	Not null	Varchar(10)
ISBN	Not null	Char(10)
State	Not null	Number(2)
Step	Not null	Number(2)

As indicated by this definition, all fields in this table must have some value assigned. The ID is a system-assigned sequential number. The order number is unique and is assigned upon submission, as is the ISBN. The State and Step values will be stored as a number representation as noted below.

States
1—Validation
2—Format
3—Proof
4—Correction
5—Production
6—Available
7—Sales
8—Termination
Steps
1—Ready
2—In Process
3—Suspended
4—End

Submission

The submission state exists only in a virtual mode. It exists from the time that a writer opens an account with RPC to the moment that a complete document (and its associated materials) is submitted to RPC.

Five sorts of data need to collected and stored for each writer. If the writer's submission is rejected by RPC, the data is stored for historical purposes only.

Data of the following types is collected and stored:

- Account data: userid and password
- Writer data: name, address, SSN, telephone, e-mail address

- Document data: title, length (in number of words), subject categories
- Marketing data: target audience, market, description, writer bio
- Document data: document files, graphics, cover

Order Table

Upon submission, an order table is created, a unique order number is assigned, and the above data is stored in the database with the order number as a key. At the same time, as we noted earlier, a unique ISBN is assigned to the document, and the global State-Step table is updated with the order number, ISBN, the state is set to Validation, and the step is set to Ready.

Name	Null?	Type
ID	Not null	Number(10)
OrderNo	Not null	Varchar(10)
ISBN	Not null	Char(10)

Writer data elements
Document data elements
Marketing data elements
Document files

Validation

The validation state is entered once a document has been submitted, **and** an order table is created and an order number and ISBN number have been assigned. For each document that enters the validation state, a record is written to the validation table indicating the disposition of the document.

When a document enters the validation state, the State and Step table is updated with the step of Ready. Once validation begins, the State and Step table is updated with the step of In Progress. If the validation is successful, the State and Step table is updated with a step of End and the state is changed to Format at step Ready, otherwise the validation state step is set to Suspended.

The validation table collects data about the validation activity. For each action in the validation activity, a bit is set to Y or N (1 or 0) and a reason code is assigned, and perhaps a textual description is entered. The validation table below indicates these actions.

Validation Table

Name	Type
ID	Number(10)
OrderNo	Varchar(10)
ISBN	Char(10)
Writer data	Char(1) (Yes or No)
Writer data	Char(1) Reason code
Writer data	Varchar(4096) Text description
Document data	Char(1) (Yes or No)
Document data	Char(1) Reason code
Document data	Varchar(4096) Text description
Graphics data	Char(1) (Yes or No)

Graphics data   Char(1) Reason code
Graphics data   Varchar(4096) Text description
Market data   Char(1) (Yes or No)
Market data   Char(1) Reason code
Market data   Varchar(4096) Text description
Document files Char(1) (Yes or No)
Document files Char(1) Reason code
Document files Varchar(4096) Text description

Format

The format state is entered once a document has entered the validation state and the end step.

When a document enters the format state, the State and Step table is updated with the step of Ready. Once formatting begins, the State and Step table is updated with the step of In Progress. When formatting is completed, the State and Step table is updated with a step of End and the state is changed to Proof at step Ready. The format state may be suspended if there are problems (such as the graphics are not in the correct dpi or the graphics designer is out sick).

The format table collects data about the formatting activity. For each action, such as work on the cover, the table stores the step (ready, end, in progress, suspended). Only when all the actions for the activity have been completed and are at step End is the entire state considered to be at an end. The format table below indicates these actions.

Format Table

Name	Null?	Type
ID	Not null	Number(10)
OrderNo	Not null	Varchar(10)
ISBN	Not null	Char(10)

Cover work step
Text work step
Graphics work step

Proof

The proof state is entered once a document has entered the formatting state and the end step.

When a document enters the proof state, the State and Step table is updated with the step of Ready. Once the writer is provided with the proofs, proofing begins and the State and Step table is updated with the step of In Progress. When proofing is completed (which is indicated by the return of the proof form to RPC), the State and Step table is updated with a step of End and the state is changed to Correction at step Ready. The proofing state may be suspended if there are problems (such as the writer does not provide a proof form within the allotted time).

The proof table collects data about the proofing activity.

Proof Table

Name	Null?	Type
ID	Not null	Number(10)

OrderNo	Not null	Varchar(10)
ISBN	Not null	Char(10)

Cover available to writer
Text available to writer
Proof form available to writer
Scheduled end date
Proof form returned

Correction

The correction state is entered once a document has entered the proof state and the end step.

When a document enters the correction state, the State and Step table is updated with the step of Ready. Once the corrections are provided to the proof corrector, proofing begins and the State and Step table is updated with the step of In Progress. When correction is completed, the State and Step table is updated with a step of End and the state is changed to Production at step Ready. The correction state may be suspended if there are problems (such as the writer has more corrections than are allowed or wants extensive corrections and so on).

The correction table collects data about the corrections activity. Only when all the actions for the activity have been completed and are at step End is the entire state considered to be at an end. The correction table below indicates these actions.

Correction Table

Name	Null?	Type
ID	Not null	Number(10)
OrderNo	Not null	Varchar(10)
ISBN	Not null	Char(10)

Number of corrections
Cover correction step
Text correction step
Graphics correction step

Production

The production state is entered once a document has entered the correction state and the end step.

When a document enters the production state, the State and Step table is updated with the step of Ready. Once production begins, the State and Step table is updated with the step of In Progress. When production is completed, the State and Step table is updated with a step of End and the state is changed to Available at step Ready. The production state may be suspended if there are problems.

The production table collects data about the production activity. Only when all the actions for the activity has been completed and are at step End is the entire state considered to be at an end. The production table below indicates these actions.

Production Table

Name	Null?	Type
ID	Not null	Number(10)
OrderNo	Not null	Varchar(10)
ISBN	Not null	Char(10)

Cover ready for print
Text ready for print
Graphics ready for print
Printing parameters set
File stored for printing

Availability

The available state is entered once a document has entered the production state and the end step.

When a document enters the available state, the State and Step table is updated with the step of Ready. Once availability begins, the State and Step table is updated with the step of In Progress. When availability is completed, the State and Step table is updated with a step of End and the state is changed to Sales at step Ready. The available state may be suspended if there are problems.

The available table collects data about the availability activity. Only when all the actions for the activity has been completed and are at step End is the entire state considered to be at an end. The available table below indicates these actions.

Available Table

Name	Null?	Type
ID	Not null	Number(10)
OrderNo	Not null	Varchar(10)
ISBN	Not null	Char(10)

In Books in Print
Booksellers informed
Web site set up
Distributor informed
Sales order processing set up
Author's copies printed
Marketing has begun

Sales

Until the book contract is terminated, the book enters and remains in the sales state.

When a document enters the sales state, the State and Step table is updated with the step of Ready. Once sales begin, the State and Step table is updated with the step of In Progress. When the contract is terminated, the State and Step table is updated with a step of End and the state is changed to Termination. The sales state may be suspended if there are problems.

The sales table collects data about the sales activity.

Sales Table

Name	Null?	Type
ID	Not null	Number(10)
OrderNo	Not null	Varchar(10)
ISBN	Not null	Char(10)

Sales order number
Sale date
Sale price
Quantity
Discount

Termination

Unless renewed, a book enters the termination state when its contract expires or for any other valid reason. This state has no steps.

The termination table stores information about terminations.

Termination Table

Name	Null?	Type
ID	Not null	Number(10)
OrderNo	Not null	Varchar(10)
ISBN	Not null	Char(10)

Contract start date
Contract end date
Termination date
Termination reason
Termination comments

Data Views or Reports

For each of the state tables described in the previous sections, there will be a corresponding tabular report. Since each report displays data about items in a specific state, each report is in effect a single state machine and a single application. That being the case, the RPC POD system will be implemented as a set of applications, each with its own application window.

Users will access the RPC POD system through an application window for each state that displays a state report. Put another way, each state will have a corresponding application window in which a report will be displayed. Each application window (and its corresponding report) will have a specific set of menus and commands that are used to process items in a specific state. These reports and state-specific commands are described in the section on the user interface.

Each state's application window will have the standard Windows File, Edit, Window, and Help menus displayed as a matter of course. In addition, each such application window will have one or more application-specific menus. The standard Help menu will have only the About topic and a command to access the IDM support facility. No general help will be provided. Instead, each application window will have context-specific help associated with every focus item on the screen.

User Management

As described in detail in the following section on the user interface, no user will have access to the "whole" RPC POD system as such. Each user will, instead, have access to the system through a report that displays data from a state table.

When a user logs in to the RPC POD system using the standard userid and password mode of authentication, this will provide access to a report. To control who has access to what reports, each user will also be assigned to a group that is defined by a system state. If a user belongs to a group, that user simultaneously has access to the report or reports available to users who work on a book in that state.

For example, a person who works on creating covers will belong to the format group. If that person also works on corrections, then the correction group will also be included. An order taker, on the other hand, would belong to the sales group. A member of management may belong to the global group and the termination group, but may be excluded from all other groups since one rarely wants management messing around with formatting or production.

Upon login, the system will check for group membership and provide access to those reports that are viewable to members to the group or groups in which the user belongs. Access authentication will thus check for a valid userid, a valid password, and a valid group assignment.

User Interface

The RPC POD will be implemented as a small set of FSMs using the graphical user interface of the Windows environment. Windows is one of the non-negotiable demands of RPC for their system. As is to be expected in the Windows environment, IDM will use the standard Windows capabilities such as applications windows for the application system and the standard WIMP factors (windows, icons, menus, and the use of a pointing device such as a mouse).

IDM proposes to use a number of different application windows with one window for each state identified in the RPC process. One window will provide management with an overview of the entire RPC process. In addition, each state as described above will be provided with its own application window. The result will thus be a set of application windows, each with its own set of applicable menus (and commands), icons and windows.

Global View of the RPC Process

All users who belong to the management group (see the previous section) will have access to a global report that shows the number of items in each state (and step within a state). This will permit these users to know at a glance what is happening in the RPC process.

The global report will be implemented as a table and will resemble a spreadsheet with a few rows. Upon logging onto the system, anyone in the management group will see this report. Bottlenecks and other problem areas will be visible at a glance and action can be taken to move personnel to these and other problem areas.

The report will have a cell for each state and all states will be shown, left to right, in their processing order. Each cell will show five items of information. At the top of the cell will be a count of the total number of items in the state. Below will be rows that show the number of items in each step within a state. So, a cell will have a format that looks like this:

Books in X State: nn
Ready: nn
In Progress: nn
Suspended: nn
End: nn

The first row in the example above will have its values retrieved by an SQL statement in the form:

SQL> select count from StateStep where state=*state*

Subsequent rows in the cell will have its values retrieved from the StateStep table with an SQL statement in the form:
SQL> select count from StateStep where state=*state* and step=*step*

If we instantiate the format with realistic values, the Validation state, for example, would look like this:

Books in Validation State: 23
Ready: 12
In Progress: 10
Suspended: 1
End: 0

A report like this would instantly inform the manager or process supervisor that there are 12 books that are ready for the validation process to kick off (manually or automatically), 10 that are in progress, and one that has been suspended for some reason.

IDM proposes to let users arrange these cells in any way that they prefer, horizontally, vertically, or diagonally. So, for example, a diagonal arrangement of the global report would look something like this.

Books in Validation State: 23
Ready: 12
In Progress: 10
Suspended: 1
End: 0

Books in Format State: 9
Ready: 6
In Progress: 1
Suspended: 1
End: 1

Books in Proof State: 17
Ready: 2
In Progress: 15
Suspended: 0
End: 0

Books in Correction State: 7
Ready: 6
In Progress: 1
Suspended: 0
End: 0

The conventions for this global view will be that if a user double-clicks a cell, another report will display showing details for the books in that state. These detail reports are described, in general, in the following section. A detailed description of these detail reports and how they are used will be found in the section on documentation and system use.

Local Views of the RPC States

While the global report described above displays data about each state and step within a state (that is, it displays data collectively and distributively), the local reports will display only data for a specific state and its steps.

For example, if a user is assigned to the production group and works on production issues they would, upon login, see a report that looks like this:

ID	ISBN	Cover	Text	Graph	Params	Files
1	1111111111	RY	RY	RY	RY	RY
2	2222222222	IP	RY	RY	RY	RY
3	3333333333	End	End	End	End	RY

This report tells the logged on production user that production activity has not yet started for the first item (all steps are ready, RY), only the cover has finished for the second item, and the third item has almost completed the production activity with only a matter of loading and locking the files needed to print the book on demand left to do.

Each such state report will display not only the books that are in that state, but will provide the menu items (commands) that are necessary to perform the activities related to that state. Irrelevant commands (and menus) will not be included. This feature of the RPC POD system developed by IDM means that superfluous or irrelevant commands will not need to be searched for or remembered by the user. The user will swiftly become familiar with the small set of menus and commands that are directly relevant to performing the activity of a state and its steps.

For details on how these types of reports are used, please refer to the following section.

Documentation and System Use

This section describes how to use the RPC POD system. All users should read the general introduction; management users should read the section on global views; all other users should read the section on local state views.

General Introduction

The RPC POD system is designed to assist users in doing their jobs—not to replace the jobs. In addition, IDM has designed the system so that users will experience a minimum of confusion over what commands to activate at what points, and to enable users to have a minimal learning curve.

All (or most) of the standard Windows functionality that you are used to using is available in the RPC POD. To launch a command, you select and click it. To select an item you want to work on, select it, then select and launch the command that you want to use.

To understand how the system works, imagine the RPC process as a manufacturing process and the manufacturing tasks laid out on a long bench. Along the bench are various rest points or stops. At each stop, some work is performed on the product (in RPC's case, books) that you are manufacturing. When the tasks associated with a stop are completed, the product continues down the bench to the next work stop. At the final work stop, the book is finished and ready for sales.

—>Work Stop—>Work Stop—>

The system is implemented as a set of windows through which you can view what is going on in the RPC process.

There is a global view, described below, that managers and supervisors use to view what is going on in the entire process. Then there are local views that allow users to see what's available for work at each work stop, and that provides the tools needed to do the work required at that work stop.

So, for example, the book publishing process begins with a submission from a writer, proceeds to the validation work stop, then on to the format work stop, then the proof, correction, and production work stops, in that order. Those users who work on the format step will have a view of all work that is waiting to be done at that step and the tools (commands linked to menus) that are needed to perform that work step.

The work that is available at each work stop is shown in the local view for that work stop. Each work stop is called a state. Each state also has several steps that we call steps (like the ready step, the end step, the in process step, and the suspended step). When a user logs into the system, they will login to a specific view depending on which state they are responsible for working on. If you work on formatting, you will login to the format view; if you work in production, you will login to the production view, and so on.

The view you login to will display all the books that are available for working on in a specific state. When you are finished working on a book that is in your view, the book will disappear from your view and turn up in the view of the next state (or work stop).

Global Views

There is one top-level view in the RPC POD system and also some summary views.

Top-Level View

Whenever anyone who belongs to a management or supervisor group logs in, they will see a view (a tabular report) that looks like this:

Validation State: 23 Format State: 9...

Ready: 12	Ready: 6...
In Progress: 10	In Progress: 1...
Suspended: 1	Suspended: 1...
End: 0	End: 1...

The view will show all the states, not just the two states shown above. A manager or supervisor can see at a glance what is going on in the RPC process. Everything under the Ready step is ready for work. Everything in the end step has moved on to the next state (and someone else's work stop).

From this global view, a manager can see at a glance if there are bottlenecks anywhere. Consider the following data that is shown for the correction state (the state after you get back a proof form from a writer):

Correction State: 22

· Ready: 21

In Progress: 1

Suspended: 0

End: 0

Now, depending on your situation, and what the rest of the global views look like, it might seem as if there is a lot of correction work to be done, most of which is still in the Ready step, which means that no work has yet begun to be done on it. If there is a state that shows little work that needs doing and if the person working that step is competent in correction, a manager would move that person to work on the correction view's queue of work.

If a manger wants additional details about a state, just select and click the first line (Books in such-and-such a state) and the local view (described below) for that state will display. Normally, we do not want managers to stick their fingers in people's work, so all managers can do at this point is view the information in a local view, but they cannot, unlike other users, do work on the items in the view. Of course, the system can be set up so they can do the work if they want to (it's just a simple change by the administrator), but it's generally better if managers keep their cotton picking hands off the work.

Summary Views

There are two places in the flow of the system where revenue enters the picture—when documents are submitted, and when sales are made on the finished products, books. Management will most likely want a summary report showing the revenue streams by day, week, month and year for both of these.

Management may also want time and motion summaries of the amount of time a document spent in each state (and step within a state).

Local State Views

There is a local view for each state (work stop) in the RPC process. Along with a userid and password, each user has been assigned to one or more work groups. Each group has access to a specific state view and can work on the books in that state. If you have been assigned to more than one group, then the views for those groups (or states or work stops) will be displayed in a minimized window. Just restore the view you want to work on at the moment.

Validation View

The validation state is entered when a writer has made a complete submission to RPC. The validation activity is almost totally automated, so all a user who works on this step needs to do is to examine the view to see if there are any problems. When an item has been validated, the book goes into the next state.

The validation view is shown below.

ID	Order	ISBN	Writer	Doc	Mkt	Graf	Files
1	001	1111111111	OK	OK	OK	OK	IP
2	002	2222222222	OK	SUS	OK	OK	SUS

Notice that there are two orders. One order is almost through the validation process, and only uploading the files into the appropriate directory and moving it into the format queue is in progress (IP). The other order was suspended at the point on the documents and, consequently, on the files (for you can't upload files until everything has been validated OK).

Select (highlight) the second item. You see that a menu has been activated on the window:

Order menu:

- View Writer
- View Doc
- View Mkt
- View Files

Select the View Doc item on the menu and you will see a display of the reasons why the validation of the document was suspended (SUS). Notice that an e-mail (or snail mail) has been sent to the writer specifying the reason and requesting a change before uploading the document files again.

Depending on the RPC policies, you may want to follow-up the e-mail with an e-mail of your own, or remind yourself to monitor that writer's progress in revising the document files (the document may have had fewer words than RPC allows, for example).

Format View

The format view shows all book files that have been validated successfully and are now ready for the formatting activity. The format view is shown below.

ID	ISBN	Cover	Text	Graphics
1	1111111111	RY	RY	RY
2	2222222222	IP	END	IP

Notice that the first item shows RY (Ready) for all columns. This means that no work has begun for the first item. The second item, however, shows that the cover and graphics are IP (in progress) and that text formatting is complete. Notice also that there are no menus on this window.

Now, select the second item. An application-specific menu now appears on the window. This means that you can use the commands on the menu, except for the Text command which has been grayed out, to work on the selected item.

Format menu

• Cover

• Text

• Graphics

Select the Cover command to continue working on the cover or the graphics command to work on the graphics.

Proof View

Once the formatting step is completed, the book moves into the proof state. The proof view is shown below.

ID	ISBN	Expect	Cover	Text	Graphics	Form
1	1111111111	120101	RY	RY	RY	RY
2	2222222222	110101	IP	IP	IP	IP

The proof view shows that the first item is ready for proofing (RY), but the writer has not yet downloaded the proofs for review. The proof form is due back on 12-01-01. The second item, however, shows IP, which means that the writer has downloaded the files for review with an expected date of 11-01-01. If the expect date passes without hearing from the writer, the date cell will change to a red color font and the step for each item will change automatically to SUS for suspended that will alert you to an unusual condition and the need for action, such as sending the writer an urgent e-mail, canceling the order, or whatever.

Correction View

Books enter the correction state when the writer has returned the proof form and corrections can begin.

ID	ISBN	CvCor	TxtCor	GrfCor	Cov	Txt	Grf
1	1111111111	2	17	6	RY	RY	RY
2	2222222222	0	12	2	END	IP	RY

The correction view shows the number of mistakes in need of correction for each element, and indicates the step at which the cover, text and graphics corrections stand. You use the same commands as in the format view to make the corrections.

Production View

Books enter the production state when the book has been formatted and all formatting corrections have been made and signed off on by the writer. The production view is shown below.

ID	ISBN	Cov	Txt	Grf	Files
1	1111111111	RY	RY	RY	RY
2	2222222222	END	IP	IP	RY

This view shows that the first item is ready for processing. The cover production is completed for the second item, the text and graphics are in progress, and the final printing files have not yet been created. Like the menus for the previous two views, there is a cover, text, and graphics command on the menu for this view, plus a files command.

Availability View

Books enter the availability state when all production is completed and books are ready to be printed on demand by the printer.

ID	ISBN	BIP	BKS	Web	SOP	Cop	Mkt
1	1111111111	RY	RY	RY	RY	RY	RY
2	2222222222	END	IP	RY	IP	IP	IP

The availability view shows that no processing has been done on item one. For item two, however, books in print (BIP) has been notified, booksellers are in process of being informed, a Web site has not been set up, sales order processing (SOP) is in progress, copies have been ordered for the writer, now author, and marketing is in progress. Upon selecting a row for processing, the window will display a menu of commands.

Sales View

The sales state is entered when the first copy of the book is sold. For each book order, a row is added to the view.

ID	ISBN	SON	Price	QTY	Total
1	1111111111	001	10.00	2	20.00
2	2222222222	002	20.00	1	20.00
3	2222222222	003	20.00	10	200.00
4	1111111111	004	10.00	7	70.00

Termination View

The termination state is entered when the contract between RPC and the writer reaches its end date, or when a contract is terminated for any other reason.

ID	ISBN	Start	End	TrmDate	Reason Comments
1	1111111111	010102	010105		
2	2222222222	090101	090104		

Notice that each ISBN has a start date and an end date. The end date and the termination date may or may not be the same. If the ISBN is at the end date, the term date is set for that date as well. If a contract terminated when it had expired, the reason would be EXP. If a contract is terminated before its end date, the end date and the term date will be different and the reason would be entered for this termination as something other than expired. Comments may also be entered.

Examples and References

A reader who is well versed in the literature of computing will know that the fastest growing design methodology for real-time systems is what is called the **workflow** methodology. Invented in the mid-1990's, workflow design is the current best implementation of the fire paradigm of design.

In this section, you will find a few URLs for enterprises or individuals engaged in the development of workflow concepts, tools or applications. I am providing these links for illustrative purposes only. I do not intend any implication that I endorse or recommend any of the following.

- **www.wfmc.org**. This is the URL for the workflow management coalition (of over 200 companies) whose mission is to (1) Increase the value of customers' investment in workflow technology, (2) Decrease the risk of using workflow products, and (3) Expand the workflow market through increasing awareness of workflow.
- **www.nemesis.co.za/** connects to Nemesis Software Systems, a supplier of workflow analysis tools.

- www.idefine.com/bast.htm of IDEFine in Europe is another supplier of workflow analysis software tools.

- cne.gmu.edu/modules/workflow describes the workflow module of George Mason University.

- www.labexpertise.com/services/workflow.htm of the Laboratory Expertise Center provides workflow analysis tools.

- www.alaska.net/~sts/workflow.html develops workflow systems.

- www.workflowsoftware.com/ is included here though I am not sure what exactly these people do (it sure isn't apparent from their Web site).

- wwwis.win.tue.nl/~wsinwa/jcsc/node14.html describes workflow analysis.

- www.metasoftware.com/Products/Product Guide.htm describes several workflow tools.

- citeseer.nj.nec.com/62846.html is an article with numerous links to theoretical workflow concepts.

- www.doc.ic.ac.uk/~ctk/publications/TR-99-2-abstract.html is a good article on workflow analysis.

- www.dstc.edu.au/praxis/index.html describes some good tools by praxis for workflow.

- hsb.baylor.edu/ramsower/ais.ac.96/papers/ VALID2.htm is an article on trigger modeling.

- dmoz.org/Computers/Software/Workflow/Products/ describes software products for workflow.

- **www.printers.ibm.com/R5PSC.NSF/Web/workflow**
  describes the IBM Printing Systems Company
  Infoprint Workflow software.

Chapter 4 Explanation of the Fire and Ice Paradigms

While the orthodox approach is to explain first and illustrate later, I have reversed this pattern in this book and provided two rather detailed examples of what the ice and fire paradigms deliver in the analysis, design, and operations phases of the systems they implement. Now, with concrete examples to work with it is time to explain or describe these two different systems.

You will, or should, have noticed that the systems produced by the two paradigms (as described in chapters 2 and 3) are entirely different. What each paradigm chose to analyze and how they designed their systems contrast quite sharply. This was intentional. I wanted to make the differences apparent. I wanted the reader to see the contrast. Max Weber, the great sociologist, advanced the method of ideal types as the best method for comparative (and historical) studies. The ideal type, for him, was an analytic construct that is used as an abstract standard or measuring rod for observers to determine the extent to which something is similar to or different from something else. I have used the fire and ice paradigms as ideal types to help support the investigation into human-centered software design.

In the following sections, I shall attempt to delineate the basic characteristics of these two ideal types of software design.

The Ice Paradigm

Let's begin with the ice paradigm. There are a number of features that appear to pervade the entire system (its analysis, design and use). Applications based on the ice paradigm are:

- Absolutistic
- Hierarchic
- Mechanistic
- A-temporal
- Abstract
- Atomic
- Documentation intensive

Absolutistic

Absolutism is the name that external observers have given to a form of political organization where the executive branch assumes sweeping powers, centralizing all decision and control in a specific person or institution.

I regard the ice paradigm as an absolutistic system because it uses one application window, and includes within that window **all** the functions that the system provides. Such a system is an everything-in-one-place system. It resembles a gigantic warehouse with its inventory stored in a way that bears no resemblance to the way any one item is used but only to the most convenient way of storing the inventory. Like the cosmology of Parmenides, all possibilities (commands) are included within one static whole.

Alan Kay, one of the founders of PARC (the Xerox Palo Alto Research Center) refers to a system like that developed using an ice paradigm as a gigantic pyramid, built by thousands of workers, piling rock upon rock.[6] I see it as a gigantic block of ice, frozen, fixed, overwhelming and scary. Systems or applications that are built according to the ice paradigm generally appear monolithic—dinosaurs unsuited to their environments. In my experience, I have never used (and never intend to use) probably ninety-five percent of

---

6.   See cause-www.niss.ac.uk/ir/library/html/erm99027.html. In this interview, Kay uses the pyramid metaphor when talking about ways that software is developed to refer to software developed in a monolithic style with hundreds of developers. He contrasts this to small-team development, which may be more creative. However, I do not think the ice and fire methods of development differ in the size of their teams so much as the paradigm they use in their development efforts. Alan Kay is the inventor of SmallTalk, the technical basis for all Windowing systems such as we find in the Mac, Windows, and the Unix-based X Windows. Alan is, in effect, one of the fathers of the PC revolution.

the commands that accompany ice systems like Microsoft Word for Windows[7], Windows itself, or Corel Photo-Paint. Most of such ice systems aren't constructed to do anything useful so much as monuments to show how seemingly clever their developers are.

Hierarchic

A second feature of the ice paradigm systems is that everything is built around the concept of hierarchy. All commands are included within menus that may or may not resemble the tasks that one actually performs, and all such commands are nested within a hierarchy of menus. It follows from such a mode of organization that all tasks require the user to work down a chain of menus and commands to perform any task.

---

7. See *What's Wrong with Microsoft Windows, Word and MSN* (Lincoln, NE: iUniverse.com, October 2001) where I describe in detail the huge number of functions included in Word, which is in my opinion the most useless software application ever developed.

Bureaucratic, hierarchical organizations are all right for the military, I suppose, but the work done in the real world of business is rarely hierarchical—except in the organization chart—and is most usually of a network character. That the world of work or of the business user can be forced into a hierarchical structure is by no means obvious. Work tends to have a flat taxonomy. And when working, one does not want to have to be constantly traversing trees to get stuff (like commands to perform tasks).

Mechanistic

A third feature of the ice paradigm systems is that the system is mechanistic. The system is constructed as if it were an independently operating machine to which the user must conform rather than the other way around. While such systems may exhibit the laws and rules of the environment that created them (such as Windows), their human users are afterthoughts.

In a mechanistic system, the work that one does is explainable or describable as a mechanical process, as a series of movements—select this, and click that. Human factors experts trying to minimize the number of clicks to perform some task, as if minimizing clicks is what makes a system human-friendly, expend lots of time and effort for nothing. A mechanistic system constructed using the ice paradigm will remain mechanistic no matter how many human factors studies are made of it.

A-temporal

Another feature of the ice paradigm systems is the complete absence of temporality from the system. There are no vectors or flows in such a system. The concept of time plays no role in the design. Each command occupies the same abstract space and has the same weight as any other command. The list of commands provided in menus has no sense of time in them—commands are a-temporal entities sitting there waiting for a user to select them.

Ice systems are like geographical maps. They portray distances and positions using spatial scales, but they convey no information about how people move about within the physical spaces of those maps. It's nice to have maps that depict everywhere one may be able to go in the land, but those who use maps never use the map to see the land but to go somewhere in particular, at a particular time for a particular period of time.

Abstract

There are two known forms of knowledge known to cognitive psychologists—conceptual and perceptual. Conceptual knowledge is abstract, a-temporal and mechanistic; perceptual knowledge is concrete, mediated by the body, and inherently temporal.

The ice paradigm produces systems that appear to be almost wholly conceptual, and devoid of perceptual knowledge and understanding. For an omnipotent, omniscient being observing everything from on high, such abstraction may be all right, but for beings whose every action is rooted in a specific spatio-temporal location, that point of view serves no purpose.

The world of abstract thought is a both-and world, a world where everything is possible and there are no hindrances and impediments—and certainly no time. This is a world of logic. It is easy to construct systems of concepts in such a world, for inference follows from inference by a chain of deductive logic. We often refer to people who live this way as having their heads in the clouds because they do not account for the rough-and-tumble world of everyday work and life. And so it is for these systems constructed according to the ice paradigm—they have a conceptual coherence, but they are pains in the butt to use.

Atomic

There is a vast difference between the world of ordinary, visible experience, composed as it is of things we can touch and manipulate, and the world of physics that explains these experiences in terms of invisible radiation and the behavior of sub-atomic particles.

One of the subtle features of systems designed according to the ice paradigm is that the process of analysis, particularly task analysis, ends when the analyst has identified the invisible features of a visible phenomenon. Many, if not most, of the commands that one finds in ice systems are of an atomic nature in that their role and place in a visible task aren't intuitive or obvious. Ice systems are pervaded by these invisible, atomic commands and functions.

Just getting ready to perform a visible, organic task like writing a letter, for example, requires a great deal of effort just setting up the environment. Using a standard word processor like Word for Windows, requires the selection of styles, fonts, formatting minutiae, page size specification, and numerous other invisible or hidden or obscure parameters many of them with consequences that are unwanted or unintended and that impede the simple task of writing.

Think, for example, of the simple task of changing the settings for a hand-held device like a mouse. Under Windows, one can change scrolling, pointers, buttons, button actions, touch sensitivity, edge motion, and other features of the mouse. If you've ever tried changing any of these features, you know that they result oftentimes in unwanted and unintended events. Many hours can unprofitably be spent mucking around with tools like this.

Documentation Intensive

A prominent feature of ice systems is that they require an extensive amount of documentation to use. Much of this documentation consists of procedures for finding the appropriate set of commands to use to perform a task. To do X, one must first go to the Y menu and select the A command, then to the Z menu to select the B command, then on to the W menu to select the C command and so on. Such procedures pervade the software application industry documentation. A rarely performed task requires the user to access the documentation each time the task is performed because remembering it is rarely possible or desirable.

One reason such systems are hard to use may be because of what I call the excessive need for mental maps. Think of a car. A car is like a vector—it is always pointing in the direction in which we want to go—forward. When someone gets in a car, they normally have a map, vision or intention of where they want to go and the car is pointing in the same direction. A few expenditures of energy later, the car is assisting us in fulfilling our intentions.

Now, consider an ice system. The user must carry a mental image of the actions that need to be done to accomplish the task the system supports, for example the book production process. Then a specific user must carry an image of a specific task that needs to be done (say, format a document into a book). Further, the user has to carry a mental image of the system that supports doing that task. Here we have three different mental constructs, at least, that must be borne in mind at the same time by the user—and all three do not mesh in any harmonious manner like the car and driver. The system has no vectors—there is nothing in an ice system that even hints at before and after or directionality of processing.

Every time I sit down in front of an application constructed according to the ice paradigm, I always have to spend some time trying to re-call just what it is I want to do and how I have to do it using the system. There is rarely anything even remotely intuitive in such system, and all generally involve heavy cognitive efforts at recall and activity.

The Fire Paradigm

The fire paradigm of system design gives us a world that is almost diametrically opposite to that of the ice paradigm. The features of the fire paradigm that will provide the evidence for this claim are listed below.

- Decentralized
- Flat
- Intentional
- Temporal
- Perceptual
- Organic
- Minimalist documentation

Decentralized

The fire paradigm does not use the absolutistic, centralized, all-in-one place approach of the ice paradigm. Instead of one central location (one application window) where all possible commands are included, we have a dispersal of function in the fire system. Each user is presented with data relevant to one state and one set of activities—and the commands included on the application window for that state are those that are appropriate only to that set of activities and that state.

Fire systems are not monolithic, centralized systems. They do not put every conceivable command on one application window. Rather, they first conceive of applications as a flow of work, then they divide the application into a set of discrete applications (finite state machines), then they provide only those commands needed to perform work on items in that state. Tasks are dispersed.

Whereas ice systems put a heavy load on the user to remember what commands are relevant for any one task and where to find the relevant commands amidst the often illogical and confused menus, the fire paradigm requires virtually no memory and little searching. If the window the user has open is to the state of formatting, for example, then only those books in that state are visible in the window and only those commands needed to perform the activities of formatting are available.

Flat

The way that a system designed according to the fire paradigm organizes its commands is flat instead of hierarchical. Each user is presented with a window (or screen) that displays the items (books) that are in a specific state and step within that state. And each window provides the user viewing that window only with the commands that are appropriate to that state and step. We do **not** see any hierarchy. In fact, though the commands may be grouped by a window-specific menu, even that grouping could be eliminated, for the items on the menu bar could point only to the small set of commands that are appropriate at the state and step in question.

The benefit of a flat taxonomy is that commands aren't forced together into some hierarchical tree, and as a result, there is no path that one has to follow to execute a command or to perform some task. It is almost as if each command is an individual object that is used to perform a specific function on the selected item (a book).

Intentional

Another feature of the fire paradigm of design is that the user is the center of the analysis and design functions.

The key feature of human action is that it is intentional—it has an aim, a purpose or a reason. Any tool (like the computer) that is meant to support or assist human users **must** make the intentionality of action a key feature of design. What does the user do at this point—not in general, not in some a-temporal universe, but at this point, now? What does a user need to do the task that is presently on the plate? What is going on right **now**, and how does one respond to it?

All human action is intentional, goal-oriented, and time-phased. Reality is process. Work is process. The **flow** of time and work is a given. Events have meaning, if at all, only because of how they affect the flow of work in time. A software application that fails to be driven and organized by events, by time, by flow, is devoid of human relevance.

Temporal

The sequential presentation of screens implies a further feature of the fire paradigm of design, namely that time is a key organizing principle. We have seen that the ice system is devoid of temporal references of any kind. The ice system provides the user at any one time with **all** of the possible commands that could be used at **any** time whatsoever. The fire paradigm, by contrast, provides the user with a temporally limited set of commands that are relevant only to the context that the user is working in at that point. This is the way the real world works.

A system designed according to the fire paradigm is one in which there is an overall sequence to the commands and windows. A management user may see at a glance what all books in each state is doing, but a worker user sees the details only at the state that he or she is responsible for working on. So, each user type gets a sense of the progression, a sense of the flow of work.

When you have used a command in a fire system, you have a sense of where you were coming from (the previous state or step in the current state), where you are now (working on items in the current state), and where the items you are working on are headed (for the next state). You thus have a sense of duration and succession (that is, of time). An ice system, by contrast, never gives one any sense of duration or succession.

A fire system thus assumes a sequential shape, like a vector or like a car, and the user has no problems orienting to the tasks at hand, for the application window displays the tasks that need to be done at that point and none other. One could compare an ice system to one where the windscreen on a car presents all possible scenes at the same time, leaving it up to the user to select the relevant scene for the moment, while a fire system presents the users with **only** what is relevant at the time. And this is how it is in real life. At each step of my way in my everyday life, I am never presented with all conceptual or logical possibilities of action at the same time—I am presented only with what is relevant to my **current** context.

Perceptual

All of the features that we have mentioned so far are features that fall under perceptual knowledge, knowledge based on perception rather than conception. Where the ice paradigm puts everything on the conceptual—and abstract—level, the fire system places everything on a perceptual level—on the level of perceptions of real events and real actions that need to be taken.

While conceptual knowledge is primarily mental, perceptual knowledge is rooted in the physical being, in the senses. Whereas conception could take place in a disembodied being, perception requires an embodied being, a being rooted at a particular place and time and responding to events at that time and place. Whereas the ice paradigm relies on conception, seeing the world in mental images laid out in an a-temporal spatial field, the fire paradigm is based on a perceptual model where the images are as much kinesthetic as mental. And since the ice paradigm is disembodied, it is also a-temporal and divorced from a context. The fire paradigm, by contrast, is firmly rooted in the here and now.

Organic

While an ice system tends to reduce commands and tasks to an atomic, invisible level, the fire paradigm, while not unaware of the invisibles also tends to re-assemble or re-compose tasks decomposed into atomic functions back into more organic, visible functions.

The tasks (activities) that one performs in a workflow system are natural or intuitive. The items are in a specific state (an a specific work queue) can be worked on in a small number of ways—and the commands made available for a state are small in number and clear as a bell to a user. Create a cover, format the text, integrate the graphics are the three main commands in the formatting state, for example. These organic commands may have atomic level sub-functions, but the atoms are subordinate to the organic command rather than the main ingredients of the command as they are in ice systems.

Minimalist Documentation

Fire systems are much less documentation intensive than are ice systems. Whereas ice system documentation spends an inordinate amount of time documenting the procedures just to find the commands one wants to use for a task, fire systems require no such elaborate procedures. This is the result of putting context-specific commands on application windows and no other. There is thus no need for elaborate command-locating procedures. Documentation can thus concentrate on describing how to use the easily findable commands.

Where an ice system requires that the user keep at least three mental images in mind for each task—the image of the time the task is to be performed, the image of the location and sequence of the commands in the application, and the image of the way to apply the commands—a fire system requires none of these. The image of the time a task is to be performed is not necessary because the application window displays only those items (like books) that can be acted upon right now in this context. The image of the location and sequence of commands is not needed because only those commands relevant to the items in the current state are available on the screen and these are always few in number and never nested in some hierarchy. And the image of the way to apply the commands is not needed because accessing the command is equivalent to running the command.

Fire versus Ice

Having considered an extended example of each of the two paradigms of fire and ice, and having outlined their theoretical differences, we are now in a better position to contrast and compare the two approaches to software design. Compared side-by-side, we can more clearly see their differences.

Ice	Fire
Absolutism	Dispersed Control
Hierarchism	Flat taxonomy
Mechanism	Intentional
A-temporal	Temporal
Conceptual	Perceptual
Atomic	Organic
Extensive Doc	Minimalist Doc

It is a normal reaction to ask if these two fundamentally different approaches to software design can be triangulated or synthesized in some way. However, observation of the stark differences as outlined above should give us pause. These are **not** merely different views like tastes; this is not Thai cuisine versus Chinese.

Whether or not someone designs software using the axioms of the ice paradigm (absolutism, hierarchism, mechanism, a-temporalism, atomism and conceptualism) or the axioms of the fire paradigm (dispersed control, a flat taxonomy, intentionality, temporalism, organicism and perceptualism) is **not** just a matter of taste or idiosyncratic preference. Underlying these two approaches to software design are fundamental philosophic principles, and determining which approach to take is subject to disputation and argument.

Triangulation or synthesis is thus out of the question. These two paradigms of software design are not mere logical contraries—where some like it hot, some like it cold, and some like it nine days old—but contradictions. Underlying these paradigms are incompatible belief systems.

If you believe that computer applications are assisting creatures that are abstract, a-temporal, mechanistic, hierarchically controllable, and need absolutistic, centralized control, then develop your applications using the ice paradigm.

If, on the other hand, you believe that computer applications are intended for the use of creatures that are primarily perceptual, temporal and intentional, with localized and contextualized activities, then develop your applications using the fire paradigm.

Fire and ice are incompatible paradigms of software design. Whereas an ice system would regard information, for example, simply as the transmission of signals through some medium, a fire system regards information as a signal that rules out possibilities. Whereas ice systems revel in the invisibilities, fire systems offer us visibilities. While ice systems view functions and tasks as static entities located in some abstract space, fire systems locate tasks and functions directly in the concrete time of work flowing from activity to activity.

Towards Human-Centered Software

A machine is a device that is supposed to lessen the amount of force required to perform a unit of work. The classical formula, work=force x distance may not work exactly in the computerized world, but it is useful nonetheless.

A computer application should help a user to do something better than that user could do the job when unaided by a computer. The degree of effort (force) and the amount of time required to perform a task using a computer application should be less than the effort and time required when unaided by a computer application.

Ice systems may be conceptually elegant and totalistic, but they do not assist users so much as they hinder and burden them. How many computer application systems are there out there that are so burdensome and cognition-intensive that they are pains in the butt to use? And why have users put up with deficiencies like that?

All of us who have used a computer (about a billion of us by now) **know** that their promise far outweighs what they deliver. We all know that there are flaws in these systems—not bugs, not things that don't quite work, but flaws, deficiencies that are rooted in the core way these things are designed to function.

To me, the fundamental flaw in software applications is not technology limitations (though it may be that too), nor is it hardware limitations (though, again, it may be that), and it is definitely not the users. The view expressed in this book is that the prime flaw in all software applications systems is the top-level principle of organization that is used to design such systems.

The principle of organization is the fundamental axiom in design. This axiom may be based on one or the other of the two fundamental categories of our cognitive consciousness—time or space. Which one we select determines how the user interface is organized and where the fundamental slices of the functional pie are made.

Businesses and other enterprises that purchase or develop software can spend an eternity doing task analyses and involving human factors agents in software development work, but that will not bring them one iota closer to human-centered software, in my opinion.

What affects human-centered software is not whether or not task analyses were done or human factors experts were involved in the development process, but whether or not a fire or an ice paradigm was used in the design of the system. The ice paradigm produces applications whose root principle of organization is a-temporal space. The fire paradigm, on the contrary, uses time as a principle of organization.

Designing computer application systems that are human-centered and that are to be used by human beings **must** thus be done using a fire paradigm. Applications developed for human beings must be time-phased or time-based. Human-centered applications are context-sensitive. Human-centered applications are ones where the work flows.

About the Author

Derek Kelly, who is retired, spent a dozen years teaching at the university level followed by twenty-five years working mainly as a technical writer in the software development industry. He has worked on teams developing applications for manufacturing process, direct mail, print on demand, human resource information, financials and other systems working on both mainframe and PC platforms.

He has published several other books including *Documenting Computer Application Systems* and *What's Wrong with Microsoft Windows, Word and MSN,* which was published by iUniverse.com in October 2001. He is currently working on a book describing a radical reconstruction of US foreign and domestic policy in light of September 11, 2001. Derek Kelly holds a doctorate from Boston University. He lives in Aurora, Colorado. He can be reached via e-mail at andrompyx@aol.com.

Index

Absolutistic, 95-96, 103, 111
Activity analysis, 57-58
Amazon.com, 19-20
APL, xi
Application window, 25-26, 29, 74, 76, 96, 103-104, 107, 109
Atomic, 95, 100-101, 108, 110
Brown, Robert Goodell, xi
CMCS, xi
Corel, 50, 97
Data element analysis, 25
Flat, 98, 103-105, 110
Function analysis, 16
GUI, 25
Heraclitus, xxxiii
Hierarchy, 97, 105, 109
Human-centered computing, ix, xii
Human-centered design, ix, xiii
Human factor, 35, 46, 98, 113
IBM, xi, xii, xvii, 5, 93
Ideal type, 94, 95
Infoprint Workflow, 93
Intentionality, 105, 110
Java, 63

Kay, Alan, 96
Kuhn, Thomas S., xix
Mechanism, 110
Menus, 25-27, 29-30, 74, 76, 80, 82, 87, 89, 97-99, 104
Microsoft, 5, 25, 50, 97, 115
Oracle, 37
Organic, 101, 103, 108, 110
PARC, 96
Parmenides, xxi-xxiii, 96
SQL, 22, 37-46, 77
STSC, xi
Stuart, Tony, xi
System analysis, 0, 12-13, 46, 51-52
Task analysis, 16-17, 35, 100
Temporal, 99, 103, 106, 110-111
Trigger, 54, 57, 92
User analysis, 13, 58
User interface, 6, 74-76, 113
User management, 13, 25, 27, 75
Weber, Max, 94
WIMP, 25, 76
Windows, 5, 25, 27, 29-32, 49-50, 74, 76, 81, 96-98, 101, 106, 109, 115
Word for Windows, 97, 101
Workflow, 53-54, 57-58, 91-93, 108
Workflow analysis, 53-54, 57, 91-92
Xerox, 96
XHTML, 18, 30, 55

www.ingramcontent.com/pod-product-compliance
Lightning Source LLC
Chambersburg PA
CBHW051246050326
40689CB00007B/1090